MONUMENTS TO FAITH

MONUMENTS TO FAITH

UKRAINIAN CHURCHES IN MANITOBA

Basil Rotoff
Roman Yereniuk
Stella Hryniuk

The University of Manitoba Press

Printed in Canada

Design: Norman Schmidt

Illustrations: Andrea Pashniak and Dong Yang Liu

Photography: Manitoba East European Heritage Society
(unless otherwise credited)

Cover photo, figs. 1.3, 1.4, 3.1, and appendix 2: Historic Resources Branch,
Manitoba Culture, Heritage and Recreation

Figs. 1.1 and 1.2: Basil Rotoff

Cataloguing in Publication Data

Rotoff, Basil, 1927-
Monuments to faith : Ukrainian churches in
Manitoba

Includes index.
ISBN: 0-88755-621-3

1. Church architecture - Manitoba - Ukrainian
influences. 2. Church architecture - Ukraine. 3.
Churches, Catholic - Manitoba. 4. Churches, Orthodox
Eastern - Manitoba. I. Yereniuk, Roman, 1946-. II.
Hryniuk, Stella M., 1939-. III. Title.
NA5246.M3R686 1989 726'.5'097127 C89-098104-3

The authors acknowledge with thanks the assistance provided by the Ukrainian Cultural and Educational Centre's staff and readers during the research and editing of
Monuments to Faith.

The University of Manitoba Press and the authors gratefully acknowledge the support
of Manitoba Culture, Heritage and Recreation in commissioning and publishing this
volume.

CONTENTS

Preface

In l988, the Ukrainian community in Manitoba celebrated the millennium of the adoption of Christianity as the state religion in the territory now known as Ukraine. To commemorate this event, the Manitoba East European Heritage Society[1] prepared this volume, with the financial assistance of the Historic Resources Branch of Manitoba Culture, Heritage and Recreation, and with the cooperation of the Ukrainian Cultural and Educational Centre.

The distinctive architecture of the Ukrainian churches that adorn the Manitoba landscape forms a major part of the heritage of Ukrainian Manitobans. Not only have these churches been seen to define the cultural and religious character of the communities in which they stand, but, more important, they are visual and aesthetic contributions to Canada's varied multicultural society.

In 1983, the Manitoba East European Heritage Society undertook a project to document fully all of Manitoba's Ukrainian Byzantine-rite churches. Over three summers the researchers documented the architecture, history and art of forty-nine churches. This research has been used as the basis for this publication.

We show in this work that the architecture of Ukrainian churches of Manitoba is rooted in the early Christian and Byzantine traditions and that there is an uninterrupted flow of these traditions from the past to the present. Over the centuries, different regional traditions have developed in various parts of Ukraine. The Ukrainian churches in Manitoba reflect the many regional, cultural and architectural traditions of Ukraine, but at the same time they are different. In this book we explain how they are different, and discuss various examples in Manitoba.

In chapter 1 we give a brief history of the Ukrainian people and how they came to the prairies, with particular emphasis on the events that influenced Ukrainian church architecture. In chapter 2 we deal with the historic roots of early Christian and Byzantine church architecture. In chapter 3 we identify the basic types of regional church buildings in Ukraine that have served as models for Manitoba's churches. In chapters 4 and 5 we show how the traditional architectural forms were transplanted to Manitoba. In chapter 6 we examine the way in which Byzantine tradition has been evolving through the creative efforts of contemporary architects. In chapter 7 we discuss the lives and work of the builders, architects and artists of Manitoba's Ukrainian churches. We recognize that the accounts of the lives and productivity of the artists are somewhat uneven; this is so because different amounts of information were available about each of them. Discussion is more extensive about those who have become historically prominent – for example, Philip Ruh and Jacob Maydanyk – and those who are still actively pursuing their professions.

In an effort to bring some order to the diversity of Ukrainian church architectural styles, we undertook a classification of churches first in Ukraine and then in Canada. We used two major criteria: the floor plan and the exterior form. Historic Ukrainian church types were derived from an analysis of plans, photographs and descriptions of some 250 churches in Ukraine. Names were assigned to these historic types on the basis of their concentration in certain regions of Ukraine; for example, most of the churches in today's Ternopil' region of the Ukrainian Soviet Socialist Republic we called the "Ternopil'" type. In the process of identifying regional and historic types of churches we observed that no specific type was limited to one Ukrainian region nor to one historic period, making precise classification difficult.

On the basis of this classification, we assigned appropriate historical and regional type names for Manitoba churches. Sometimes we found the task of identifying types difficult because the settlers did not always build their churches according to the style of their region of origin. Often churches embodied elements of several historic or regional types, further complicating classification.

In the interest of clarity, styles that do not bear directly on the architecture of Manitoba Ukrainian churches have not been included in this work.

In the course of our research it was not possible to obtain the full names of some of the people mentioned in this work, even though every effort has been made to do so.

The spelling of Ukrainian place names in this work follows the gazetteer of the *Encyclopedia of Ukraine* published by the University of Toronto Press.

This book would not have been possible without the contribution of many people to whom the authors are indebted. Much of the field research was carried out by student assistants who perused libraries, photographed churches, interviewed people and organized the research materials. Our thanks go to If Asad, Brian Belinsky, Roman Bobrownik, Daniel Bugera, Serge Demchenko, Lucy Grzegorczyk-Davison, Orest Kinasevych, Steve Lodge-Zaparnick, Pat Kuzyk, Daralynn Monita (who also acted as an able administrator), Ottilie Murray, Natalie Picklyk, Oleh Shawarsky, Angela Smook, Greg Udod and Evan Zaleshchuk.

We wish to acknowledge the expert help of Neil Einarson, David Butterfield and Ed Ledohowski of the Historic Resources Branch, Culture, Heritage and Recreation. As well, we appreciate the kind assistance of librarians Raisa Moroz of St. Andrew's College and Luba Negrych of the University of Manitoba Architecture Library.

We greatly appreciate the support of St. Andrew's College in providing the project with a home and lending much material assistance.

Finally, we wish to thank the artists who provided us with information about themselves and their colleagues who are no longer with us; the people in many parishes who shared their memories; and the many other Manitobans, too numerous to mention, who helped us in this endeavour.

INTRODUCTION

1

THERE ARE MORE THAN 100,000 Manitobans of Ukrainian descent. They are the descendants of the successive waves of immigrants who made Manitoba their home and who brought with them an ancient and rich cultural tradition, the most visible symbol of which is the church with its cupolas. Many aspects of Ukrainian history and culture have influenced the shape and form of Manitoba's Ukrainian churches.

THE UKRAINIANS OF MANITOBA

A History

Ukraine originated in a state called Kievan Rus', which flourished from the ninth to the thirteenth centuries and which stretched from the Baltic to the Black seas and from the Danube to the Volga rivers [fig. 1.1]. It was during this period, in 988 A.D., that the rulers of Kievan Rus' accepted Byzantine Christianity from Constantinople as the official religion for their subjects. This decision had a major political and cultural influence on the development of Ukrainian civilization and its churches.

The decline of Kievan Rus' began in the twelfth century. By the middle of the thirteenth century, the weakened state fell to the Tatar hordes under Genghis Khan. The Kievan state was divided into three lands: the south-central part, which was devastated and left mostly

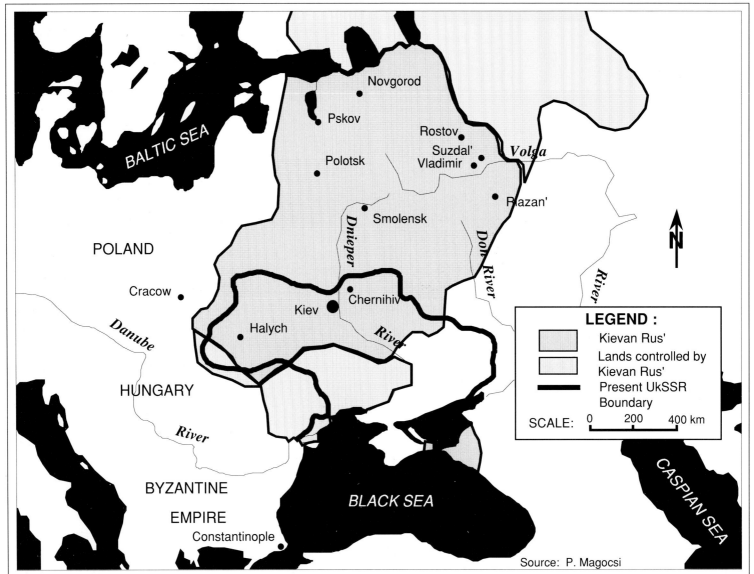

LEGEND :

▨ Kievan Rus'

☐ Lands controlled by Kievan Rus'

▬ Present UkSSR Boundary

SCALE: 0   200   400 km

Source: P. Magocsi

1.1 Kievan Rus' occupied a territory of approximately 1.2 million square kilometres, roughly twice the size of Manitoba. It also had control over an area of equal size consisting of boreal forests to the north and steppes to the south.

uninhabited; the northern parts, which later became Muscovy; and the western regions, where most of the Ukrainian people remained, and which eventually came to be dominated by Lithuania and Poland [fig. 1.2].

In the sixteenth century the Ukrainian Cossacks emerged as a distinct social class and a strong national force; they gradually wrested from Poland a degree of independence. The establishment of the Ukrainian Cossack state in the seventeenth century fostered a renaissance in education, arts and architecture.

In 1596, by virtue of the Union of Brest, some Ukrainians accepted union of the Orthodox Church with the Roman Catholic Church to form the Uniate (later the Greek Catholic and today the Ukrainian Catholic) Church. This church retained the traditional Byzantine rite but recognized the pope in Rome as its head. Hence, two churches closely related in rite – the Ukrainian Orthodox and the Ukrainian Catholic – became a part of the historic legacy that Ukrainians brought with them to Canada.

In the seventeenth century the territory of Ukraine was divided between Muscovy, Poland and the Ottoman Empire, and a century later, the Austrian Empire acquired western Ukraine (mainly the province of Galicia) from Poland, and Bukovyna from the Ottoman Empire [fig. 1.3]. During the nineteenth century, there was a growing Ukrainian national awakening, along with marked changes and improvements in the economic, cultural and political lives of Ukrainians. Finally, in the latter part of the nineteenth century, conditions arose in Austria-Hungary that encouraged a mass migration to the New World.

In the second decade of the twentieth century, Ukraine was ravaged by war, invasion and revolution; ultimately, political boundary changes resulted. Attempts to establish an independent Ukrainian national state were unsuccessful. The Ukrainian Soviet Socialist Republic (UkSSR) was established in 1920, and newly created Czechoslovakia, Romania and revived Poland became the political powers that dominated the Ukrainian lands that had previously been under Austro-Hungarian rule.

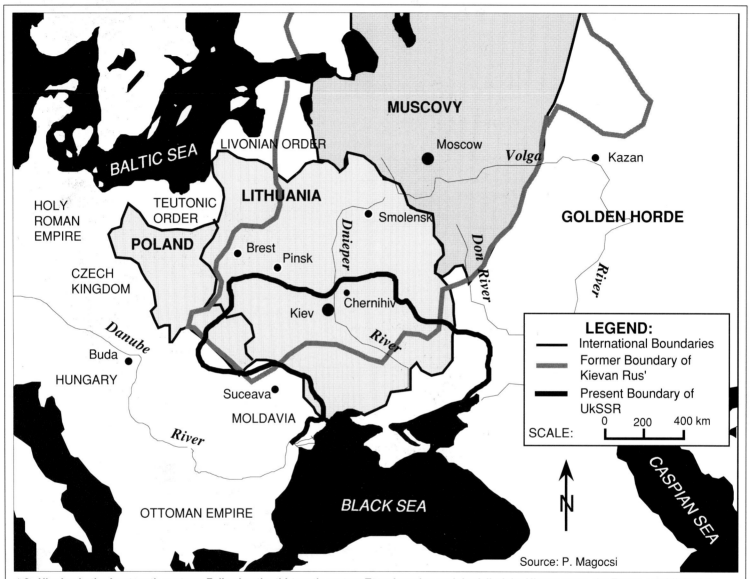

1.2 Ukraine in the fourteenth century: Following the thirteenth-century Tatar invasion and the fall of the Kievan state, the Tatars established the Golden Horde. Most of Ukraine fell under the domination of the Polish-Lithuanian Kingdom.

INTERNATIONAL BOUNDARY
PRESENT Uk.S.S.R. BOUNDARY

Scale in KM

0   100   200

N

Source: P. Magocsi

PRUSSIA

RUSSIAN EMPIRE

Smolensk

Warsaw

Brest

Chernihiv

Don River

Cracow

L'viv

Kiev

Kharkiv

Poltava

AUSTRO-HUNGARIAN
EMPIRE

Dnieper River

Danube River

OTTOMAN EMPIRE

Odessa

SEA OF
AZOV

Belgrade

Bucharest

BLACK SEA

1.3   In the eighteenth century, Poland was partitioned by Russia, Prussia and Austria. In the process, Austria acquired part of the Ukrainian lands.

The Migration to Canada

Migration to the New World changed both the migrants and the society they entered. Of the first wave (between 1891 and 1914), which was 170,000 strong, sixty-two percent settled in the three prairie provinces; they were drawn by the Canadian government's offer of 160 acres of land for a ten-dollar fee. In their European homeland, Ukrainians had been owners of small land holdings, usually less than ten hectares (twenty-four acres), which they farmed intensively and the produce of which was their main source of revenue. Most Ukrainians were good farmers; as well, they were semi-skilled craftworkers, or they participated in some domestic industry that supplemented their earnings. On their arrival in Canada, these enterprising transplanted peasants set about improving their lives.

In the 1920s there was a second wave, this one some 70,000 strong, who came largely from the same areas as did the first settlers. These immigrants settled on the Canadian prairies and in the eastern Canadian cities. A third wave came after the Second World War. This third wave was half the size of the second, and the people came from all parts of Ukraine, including western Ukraine which, after 1945, was incorporated into the UkSSR. The major difference in the character of these three waves was the more urban and non-agricultural occupational orientation of the post-1945 immigrants, and their consequent choice of settling in the urban centres rather than on the prairies.

In the settlement pattern of Ukrainians in Canada [fig. 1.4], Stuartburn, Manitoba, was the southeasternmost point of a strip of Ukrainian settlements that followed the route of today's Yellowhead Highway all the way to north-central Alberta. Clusters of families, often from the same or neighbouring counties in Galicia or Bukovyna, formed block settlements. This is a factor that contributed to the transplanting, perpetuation and preservation of the homeland language and traditions, including religious traditions. Large settlements sprang up around Stuartburn in southeastern Manitoba, Gimli in the Interlake area,

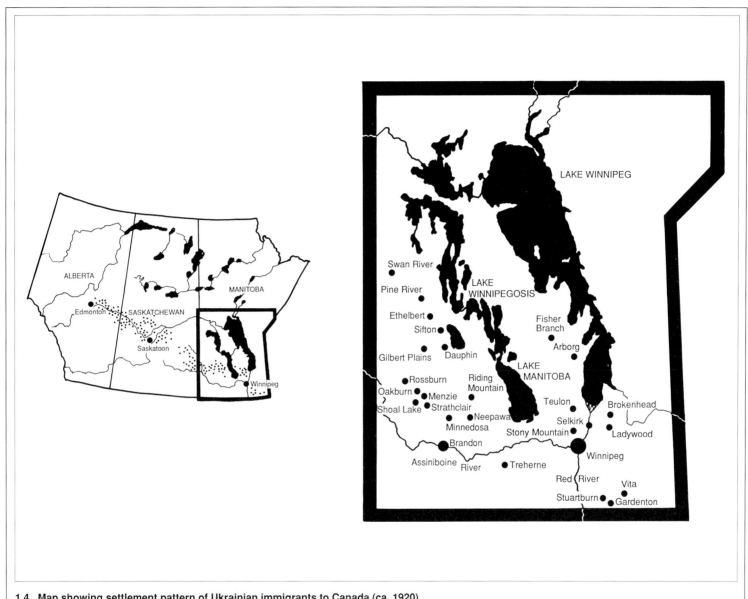

ALBERTA

MANITOBA

Edmonton SASKATCHEWAN

Saskatoon

Winnipeg

LAKE WINNIPEG

Swan River

Pine River

LAKE
WINNIPEGOSIS

Ethelbert

Sifton

Fisher
Branch

Gilbert Plains Dauphin

Arborg

LAKE
MANITOBA

Rossburn Riding
Mountain

Oakburn

Menzie

Teulon

Brokenhead

Shoal Lake Strathclair

Neepawa

Selkirk

Ladywood

Minnedosa

Stony Mountain

Brandon

Winnipeg

Assiniboine River

Treherne

Red River

Vita

Stuartburn Gardenton

1.4   **Map showing settlement pattern of Ukrainian immigrants to Canada (ca. 1920).**

in Shoal Lake, Oakburn and other towns in the area south of Riding Mountain National Park, as well as in Dauphin, Ethelbert and other areas north of the park. Moreover, in Brandon, Portage la Prairie and Winnipeg, vibrant Ukrainian communities emerged before 1914; these immigrants were employed mainly in the building trades, service industries and the construction of railways. Immigrants arriving in the inter-war period, while tending to go into different occupations than did their kinfolk who had arrived earlier, followed the same settlement pattern.

In the same way that Canadian society has changed in the years after the Second World War, so have the Ukrainian communities undergone considerable change. Rural-urban and inter-provincial migration has depleted the population in a number of rural Ukrainian settlements as well as in some urban neighbourhoods. The use of the Ukrainian language has declined considerably since 1945. Finally, membership in the Ukrainian traditional churches has declined. All these factors threaten the continuing survival of Ukrainian communities in Manitoba.

The Role of the Church
The church played a dominant role in the life of Ukrainians in their European homeland. The village church was the hub of activities – religious, cultural and, for a long time, educational. The priest was a leading intellectual and social figure in village life, providing not only spiritual guidance and pastoral care to his faithful, but also advice on improved agricultural methods, world news and political happenings.

Ukrainians in Galicia and Bukovyna led an organized parish life, forming church brotherhoods and sisterhoods to administer the practical and spiritual needs of the membership. The peasants admired and respected their clergy, and demonstrated their ardent faith in God in their devotion to the liturgy and rituals of their church. They brought this attitude to Canada where they found the religious situation to be vastly different. There were no churches nor priests familiar to them, and it was several decades before permanent Ukrainian church structures came into existence. The Ukrainian Catholic Church in Canada was established in 1912, and the Ukrainian Orthodox Church in 1918. These remain the two traditional Ukrainian churches in Canada.

MANITOBA UKRAINIAN CHURCH ARCHITECTURE AND ART

The Tradition
The churches of Ukraine were identifiable to observers because of certain architectural features. The church was built on the highest point of land in the chosen area, harmonizing with its natural surroundings, striving upwards and topped by bulbous domes. The interior was also distinguishable from other religious buildings. The church was to face the east, it was to have a square altar and usually an iconostasis (icon screen) separating the nave from the sanctuary. In Ukraine, the rich decoration of the interior varied according to the type of church it was (stone or wooden) and according to the wealth of its congregation. Traditionally, the complete wall surfaces of stone churches were covered with painted icons, or mosaics or frescoes. In wooden churches, the walls were not painted, but other decorative features were used, such as special decorative wood constructions or icons painted on wood and hung freely on the walls. Also, Ukrainians embellished church walls, pillars, ceilings, arches and pews with painted folk motifs, usually drawn from Christian symbols (*rospys*). In addition, the ceilings and domes were almost always painted blue with variously shaped stars to signify the heavenly skies. In both stone and wooden churches, the iconostasis was elaborate, with icons, wood carvings and gilding.

Iconography was a very serious art form in Ukraine, where in the early centuries of Christianity the great icon artists were masters from Byzantium who were assisted by local masters. Within the next century, these local artists became masters in their own right. The Kiev Monastery of the Caves (Kievo-Pechers'ka Lavra) was the first major centre for developing Ukrainian icon masters. Regional influences appeared very early in Ukrainian icon painting. The icon painter looked upon his work as a very special vocation, praying and fasting in preparation for the work of painting. He knew that the icons were more than mere representations or art forms. Rather, they were to be painted in a certain manner according to specific rules so that the finished icon would directly convey the holiness of the persons and feasts depicted in the icon. In the Ukrainian tradition, the icons were to provide an atmosphere of mystery and sacredness. Together with the other artwork in a church, they were to give the worshipper a sense of harmony, beauty and tranquillity – a foretaste of paradise.

In the centuries when Ukrainian lands were under the Polish-Lithuanian administration, elements of the tradition of the people crept into the building and decoration of Ukrainian churches. Especially in the urban centres in the western Ukrainian lands, the strength and proximity of the Roman Catholic Church made the entry of Latin-rite traits into Ukrainian church art inevitable. Statues, stations of the cross, holy-water fonts and paintings in the style of the Latin rite appeared in Ukrainian churches. This tendency seemed to increase in the eighteenth and nineteenth centuries before Ukrainians from Galicia began to emigrate to Manitoba. Similarly, a Russian influence was evident in churches on the Ukrainian territories in the Russian empire, especially in city churches. Many priests were trained in non-Ukrainian seminaries, and they, as leaders, often gave their own modified interpretation of the traits they admired to the churches they served, especially in the construction and decoration of the church.

The Transition to Manitoba
When Ukrainians first arrived in Manitoba they found themselves not only without churches and priests, but also without any traditional models from which they could build their first churches, without any architectural or artistic documentation from which to work, and with real economic limitations. However, they fell back on traditions of self-

reliance and did their best within their limited intellectual and material resources. They initiated the building and decoration of their first churches on their own, whether or not there was a priest to serve them. Some of the more educated people among them were neither particularly interested nor desirous of helping them design, build or decorate their churches, since many of them were anticlerical for personal or political reasons. (Anticlericalism was a significant feature of the radical political movement in Galicia, to which many young intellectuals were attracted.) When they first arrived, the Ukrainian settlers sometimes used chapels or churches in cooperation with the Poles or Romanians. The Holy Ghost Church in Winnipeg and the churches in Lennard and Oakburn are examples. This sharing led to the appearance of different influences in Ukrainian church architecture and art. A completely novel influence for Ukrainians in Manitoba was the existence of Protestant missionaries and their churches. The Protestant structures were often visibly impressive, and the Ukrainian settlers came to use similar materials for their own church buildings.

For the first few years after they arrived, the settlers would often gather for religious services in each others' houses or farmyards, using primitive outdoor or indoor altars. In time, regular attenders would decide to build a church. Volunteers provided land, materials and labour. A building committee would be formed, which in all likelihood consisted of the stalwarts in the community, who would be responsible for fund-raising and coordinating the construction and decoration of the church. If there were money already available, the committee would purchase land or lumber if need be, and undertake to raise more money to pay for further needs. To establish an architectural design, the commonest device (and one which on occasion was used as late as the 1940s), was for the committee to gather ideas and memories of the "old country" village church. This set of ideas would then serve as the building plan and would be given to the master carpenter at a committee gathering. From the records of most of the early Manitoba churches, it is clear that the supervision of construction was usually entrusted to one person called a *budivnyk* (builder), or, rarely, two people. These men performed the functions which, from the 1950s onward, were carried out by architects and engineers. The *budivnychi* were usually skilled carpenters with good local reputations. Once they had launched the construction process, all available hands in the community were called upon to help complete the task. After the building was complete, the parish members would donate the religious articles needed – the icons, altar cloths, candelabra, crosses and banners. If they did not already own such articles, they would purchase or hand-craft them.

The interior decoration of the church did not always occur immediately after the church was built. Often all that was done at first was the painting of the walls (as one would paint the walls of a house). This allowed the parish a time to pay any debts incurred and to collect money for hiring a painter-artist to enrich the ornamentation of the interior. Consecration of a new church by the bishop would take place as soon as possible after construction was completed.

In a few cases parishes decided to purchase buildings, usually churches of other denominations, rather than to build new churches of their own. In these cases only reconstruction and interior redecoration would be needed.

In the post–Second World War period, the pattern was altered quite dramatically. The movement of Ukrainians from the country into the cities, especially into Winnipeg, was a major factor. So too were the greater material prosperity of the settlers, and the influx of a new group of Ukrainians from Europe. The migration of Ukrainians into cities has enlarged their parishes, and the members found it necessary to build newer, larger structures. At the same time, rural churches have lost large portions of their congregations, and the buildings have begun to deteriorate. Some parishes, such as the Assumption of the Blessed Virgin Mary Ukrainian Catholic Parish in Portage la Prairie, have decided to demolish the older, larger structures and build newer, smaller churches. As well, largely due to their greater wealth, Ukrainian parishes have begun hiring professional architects, construction companies and artists for building and renovating their churches. The result has been that Ukrainian churches, while they are more sturdily built due to conformity with present-day building standards, have lost some of their traditional architectural and artistic elements. However, there has recently been a revival of interest in some Ukrainian parishes in restoring the traditional elements in building and decorating Ukrainian churches. For instance, the use of the iconostasis is reviving, especially in Ukrainian Catholic churches. This revival of interest in the traditional has been attributed to the post-war immigration of Ukrainians to Canada, and to greater education among Ukrainians generally about their religious traditions.

Structural Adaptations in the New Land
When the immigrants arrived in Manitoba, they were faced with two sets of conditions that had a substantial effect on the way they built their churches. First, the church had to be built for the harsh prairie climate that also seriously limited the time available for construction. Second, they soon discovered that the building materials and the techniques to which they were accustomed in their homeland were of limited useful-ness here. The natural materials that were abundant all around them in the Carpathian mountains and foothills, such as tall timber and river stone in the Ternopil' plateau land, did not exist in Manitoba. Here, good logs were scarce and almost beyond their means. On the other hand, while manufactured building materials were expensive or inaccessible in the home country, they were cheap and relatively commonplace in Canada. Sawn lumber was readily available from the local lumberyard and was relatively inexpensive; building hardware of all kinds was at their disposal, as were all sorts of prefabricated building components. As well, the creative and dynamic new world (which they themselves were helping to create) offered the advantages of labour-saving building techniques.

By the mid-1920s, a certain pattern developed in Ukrainian church building in Manitoba. The earliest settlers attempted a close replication of traditional styles, but gradually the builders adapted their work to Canadian building materials and techniques, as well as to the rigours of the prairie climate. Consequently, churches built near the turn of the century tended to be much closer to the homeland prototype than are the more recent ones, both in overall design and in structural detail.

The churches built by the settlers were much smaller than the homeland originals were. Churches in Ukraine served villages or towns often consisting of several thousand people, and there was a broad base of financing and volunteer labour. The Ukrainian communities in Manitoba, however, numbered perhaps only a few hundred people, and their churches were appropriately smaller.

The first major adaptation to Canadian conditions was the abandonment of the traditional log-and-timber construction. The very essence of the architectural style of the wooden churches of the Carpathians had been inherent in the materials used. The distinctive identity of these churches resulted not only from the visible qualities of log and timber, but also from the construction techniques necessitated by the shape and texture of log and timber. Many of the common features and details found in these buildings were an indigenous way of solving real architectural problems rather than a function of tradition. For example, the distinctive cantilevers in the corners of Lemko and Boyko churches [fig. 3.3] were an economical means of supporting the wide roof overhangs required by the climate; similarly, the tent-frame roof construction in the Hutsul churches was a way of creating a dome from primitive materials (logs and shakes). These problems no longer presented themselves with frame construction; as a result, the overall form of the building began to change, and ceased to reflect faithfully the old country models. Many of the construction details that were formerly justified by structural needs became mere token decorative motifs, considerably reduced in importance and size.

14

Soon, perhaps around the time of the First World War, builders began to realize the full potential of frame construction and the flexibility it provided. Rather than limit themselves to replicating timber churches, they began to imitate the form and texture of the stone churches of their former homeland. This was particularly evident in the churches built in the Ternopil' cruciform style[1] and the Kievan style, as well as in Fr. Philip Ruh's "prairie cathedrals." All interior surfaces in the new churches were finished in the traditional form with icon paintings and frescoes as though they were masonry. Some aspects of this adaptation were relatively simple, especially if they did not require structural treatment. For instance, a common technique was to render in paint the textures of marble and stone upon surfaces of wood or plaster. However, when the adaptation related to structural features, more imaginative solutions were required. For example, if there were an interior dome, it would be necessary to replicate as well the pendentives upon which the four evangelists are traditionally depicted (see chapter 2 and appendix 1). The pendentive is an inherent structural feature of masonry not required in frame construction. The builders had therefore to resort to various ingenious means to recreate pendentives in wood. One method was to add a small structure in the valleys created by the meeting of two gable roofs [fig. 4.17].

The fact that prefabricated materials were available also influenced the shape and form of churches. Stock sizes of plywood and lumber imposed a certain standardization of elements and dimensions. In one sense standardization made construction much easier, but in another it affected the free-form, flowing designs that characterized many of the original models. Gone were the oversized, massive oak doors, the irregular and wavy *piddashshia* with hand-worked supporting timber posts, and the miscellaneous forged and wrought-iron accessories. There were now standard heights, standard doors and windows, and standard hardware. For example, the prefabricated "prairie gothic" window, which could be found in practically any lumber supplier's or sash-and-door manufacturer's catalogue, found its way into the Eastern Christian churches of Manitoba and became widely accepted.

Very often the style of Ukrainian churches in Manitoba has been affected by the covering of the exterior walls with stucco. These churches, although originally built according to the traditional "wooden-church" style, look substantially different from them, departing even further from the homeland model. This is particularly true of churches that have in recent years been rehabilitated as "historic" structures as projects undertaken to commemorate anniversaries or community achievements. It is unfortunate that the work of rehabilitation has covered up or removed some of the more elaborate traditional ornamentation and texture; many of these churches have lost their historic characteristics.

THE SOURCES OF UKRAINIAN CHURCH ARCHITECTURE

2

THE BYZANTINE EMPIRE was the dominant state in the eastern Mediterranean basin between the fourth and fifteenth centuries, and it exerted a strong cultural influence on eastern Europe, specifically the Kievan Rus' state, the future territory of Ukraine. Hence, Ukrainian church architecture is based on Byzantine church architecture.

EARLY CHURCH ARCHITECTURE

The origin of Byzantine church architecture can itself be traced to Judaic, Syrian and Roman sources. The Jews had used the basilica form for their place of worship – the synagogue. It was rectangular in shape, usually with two rows of columns, with an apse at one end and, usually, one to three doors at the other end of the building [fig. 2.1]. Until the second or third century A.D. the doors of the synagogue always faced Jerusalem; later it became customary for the apse to be oriented toward Jerusalem.

The oldest type of Christian church building, however, was the Syrian church, in which the basilica shape of the synagogue was adopted for Christian use. The apse was no longer oriented toward Jerusalem, but rather toward the geographical east. The reading of the scriptures and prayers took place in a special area called the bema, in the centre of the nave, and the apse became the sanctuary for the Eucharist [fig. 2.2].

There are few records of the type of church built in the Roman Empire before the end of the persecutions (in the early decades of the fourth century), since Christians worshipped predominantly in home churches. The first great Christian edifices were basilicas built with the support of Emperor Constantine the Great, in the beginning of the fourth century [fig. 2.3]. This style of church architecture remained the norm for the next three centuries. It was popular for its simplicity of construction and its ability to hold large numbers of worshippers. During this time, variations were made in the interior of the basilica. Sometimes the two rows of columns and three-aisle configuration was increased to four rows of columns and five aisles [fig. 2.4], or the apse was given a polygonal rather than the more conventional semi-circular shape. By the end of the fifth century, the basilica style was used mostly in Italy.

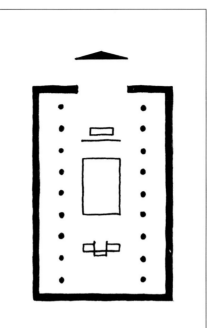

2.1 A typical synagogue building of the pre-Christian era. The reading of the scriptures and the teaching took place from the bema, at the centre.

2.2 The early Syrian church resembled the synagogue in structure. It retained the bema for the reading of the scriptures, then the presbyters would move to the apse for the sacramental part of the liturgy.

Another Roman form, the circular building, gained popularity in the fourth and fifth centuries. Circular temples had been in existence since pre-Christian times, and were now adapted for Christian use. For example, the Pantheon in Rome was converted for Christian use [fig. 2.5]. The Churches of the Nativity and of the Holy Sepulchre in Palestine also embody this style. But, however elaborate the construction, the ground plan of circular buildings imposed certain functional limitations, such as a lack of adequate space for the sanctuary and the choirs.

A major change in church architecture occurred in Byzantium in the fifth century with the development of the circular dome, which was set on a square-walled space below. Two different methods were used to support the dome. One was the squinch method, consisting of small arches spanning the corners of the square space, thus converting it into an octagonal shape onto which the circular base of the dome could be fitted [fig. 2.6]. The second was the pendentive method, consisting of triangular-shaped extensions of the dome which filled the corners of the square space to transform it into a circle [fig. 2.7]. The pendentive was by far the superior architectural method of the two.

The dome gained wide acceptance in Byzantine church architecture because of its great religious symbolism. Domes were placed on the early basilicas, some examples of which are the Church of St. Irene, which was built in 532 A.D. [fig. 2.8] and the Cathedral of Hagia Sophia, built between 532 and 537 A.D. [figs. 2.9 and 2.10], both in Constantinople. The basic plan was still that of a basilica, but with a very wide centre aisle, capped at the centre by a vast dome. In addition, smaller semi-domes were placed to the east and west of the main dome, and these served to cover the space below as well as to buttress the central dome. No finer example of this Christian architecture can be found than the Cathedral of Hagia Sophia.

The technological advances that permitted the construction of the dome also permitted the development of another architectural form: the cruciform building topped by a dome over its central space [fig. 2.11]. The cruciform-shaped building, as described by art historian D. Talbot Rice, "had a particular appeal to the more mystical aspect of Christian teaching, for it combined the emblem of the faith with something that symbolized heaven above."[1] It became a preferred model for Byzantine churches built in subsequent centuries.

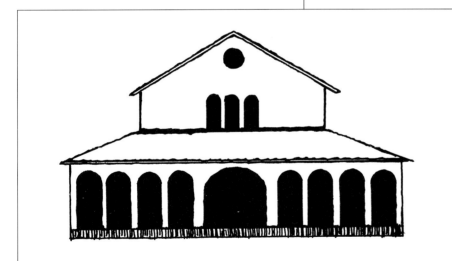

2.3 In a basilica, a row of columns would support the high part of the building, or the nave.

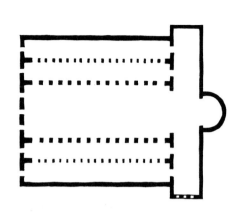

2.4 Large basilicas would have two aisles on each side of the nave. The roofline would be stepped, dropping at the inner rows of columns, then again at the outer rows.

2.5 In Roman times, the Pantheon contained statues of a multitude of pagan gods, which were placed around the circular walls of the building, facing inward. Although this type of building is still used today to glorify historical heroes (e.g., the Pantheon in Paris, the Jefferson Memorial in Washington), it proved inadequate for Christian worship.

From the middle of the ninth century onward, cruciform buildings in the Greek cross configuration became the norm. Compared with the earlier structures, the churches were now smaller, built on a more human scale. The exteriors were now decorated with blind arcades and brick-work patterns, plastering and glazed tiles. The interior walls were richly decorated with frescoes and icons. The buildings in their totality reflected the theological framework of sacred space. The dome [fig. 2.12] came to represent heaven/paradise with Christ as the Pantocrator (the Great Judge) painted on the ceiling [fig. 2.13], with the four evangelists in the pendentives. The apse became the cave of the Nativity in Bethlehem and the altar became the table of the Mystical Supper; on the walls were icons of saints and martyrs (holy figures) representing persons that had lived dedicated Christian lives.

The first Christian churches in Ukraine were built by the Greeks who colonized the northern shores of the Black Sea and Crimea from the

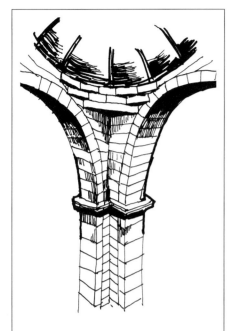

2.6 The squinch is a small arch spanning diagonally across a corner to provide a transition from a square base to a circular dome.

2.7 The pendentive is a downward extension of the curve of the dome between the arches upon which the dome itself is supported. The icons of the four evangelists are usually found there, with cherubim at the very tip of the pendentive.

second to the eighth century A.D. The colonists of this era were familiar with classical Greek and Roman architectural forms, and were later influenced by Byzantine church architecture. All the basic forms of churches were represented: the Greek cross, the basilica, the circular church and the single-nave church. A local variation of the cross-shaped plan, with a central dome and additions resembling a three-nave basilica, developed in this region. By the tenth century, when Christianity became the state religion of Kievan Rus', the Byzantine church building was already an established architectural form.

The most common building technique used in Crimea is known as *opus mixtum*, which consisted of alternating layers of squared stones and bricks held together by a mixture of mortar and powdered brick. The interior walls were built of flat brick on thick layers of mortar and had inlaid clay vessels which served as sound amplifiers. The outside walls were covered with rose-coloured mortar and painted over in red and yellow. The window openings were covered with frames containing square pieces of glass. Some parts of the roof were tiled. The altar floor was marble; the other floors were covered with glazed ceramics or were simply painted. The *opus mixtum* method was common in the construction of churches until the eleventh century. However, very few examples of structures built prior to the Christianization of Kievan Rus' survived destruction when the Tatars ravaged the land in the thirteenth century.

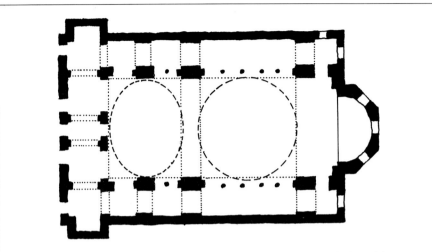

2.8   The floor plan of the Church of St. Irene shows the gradual evolution of the basilica towards a purely Byzantine configuration. Converted to a mosque, the church still stands in Istanbul.

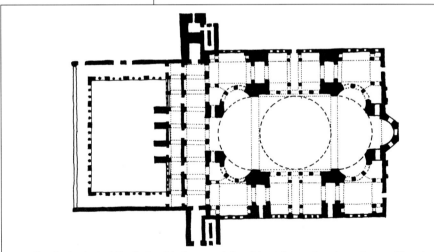

2.9   The Cathedral of Hagia Sophia is one of the oldest, largest and most magnificent Christian structures ever built. Converted to a mosque at the fall of Constantinople (1453), it is now a museum.

2.10 This is the way the Cathedral of Hagia Sophia looked before the addition of minarets by the Ottoman Turks.

2.11 The Greek cross configuration became the most common for all Eastern Christian churches.

2.12 The central dome became the most distinctive feature of Eastern Christian churches.

2.13 Christ Pantocrator (the Great Judge), as seen by one looking up into the dome.

KIEVAN CHURCH ARCHITECTURE

Very soon after the acceptance of Christianity from Byzantium, the Byzantine domed-cruciform style of church was adopted in the Kievan State. Subsequently, beginning with the late tenth and early eleventh centuries, it spread throughout central and eastern Ukraine. Kievan builders were often trained in the Byzantine style and, consequently, the Byzantine influences remained very strong, especially in their earlier work. The predominant type of structure was essentially based on the Byzantine cross-domed plan, with three naves, three apses and six columns that supported the central dome. In the eleventh century, Prince Yaroslav the Wise (1036–1054) commissioned

2.14 The Church of the Tithe, the first stone church in Kiev, was built in the tenth century. The section (a), and the plan (b), were reconstructed on the basis of archaeological research. The circles indicate the probable location of domes.

the building of a number of grand churches, all emulating the magnificent architectural style of Byzantium; but at the same time certain variations were making their appearance. Kievan building masters were beginning to introduce changes in keeping with local tastes, local building practices and, perhaps, their own creativity. These changes marked the beginning of an architectural style known as the Kievan School. In the middle of the twelfth century, a Western traveller visiting Kiev reported that it was truly a city of churches – it had some 400 of them. Kiev thus became one of the most important centres of Byzantine church architecture among these newly Christianized slavic peoples.

Few churches of the period remain, and most of the knowledge about them has been derived from archaeological research. There are a number of excellent examples. The Church of the Tithe [fig. 2.14] was built in 996 by Prince Volodymyr, who donated one tenth of his income for its construction; it was razed by Batu Khan, son of Genghis Khan, in

1240. The Church of the Assumption, built between 1073 and 1078 and rebuilt in baroque style between 1695 and 1722, was destroyed during the Second World War, but is well documented in pictorial records [fig. 2.15]. The preserved Church of Our Saviour in Berestiv, built between 1113 and 1125, is another good example of the architecture of the Kievan School [fig. 2.16].

Undoubtedly the most important church of this period was St. Sophia's Cathedral in Kiev [fig. 2.17]. Although the architecture of the cathedral is Byzantine in style and sophistication, it has features that are unique to the Kievan School. It is a five-aisled structure topped by thirteen domes, enclosed by two rows of open galleries on each side. The features that set St. Sophia's, in its original form, apart from Byzantine churches were the elongated proportions of the domes, which were raised on taller drums[2], the more marked stepped arrangement of masses, the presence of two rows of open galleries, the two towers in the west section of the cathedral, and the profusion of

2.15 Church of the Assumption at the Kievan Caves Monastery (Kievo-Pechers'ka Lavra), as it looked in the seventeenth century, prior to the baroque renovation.

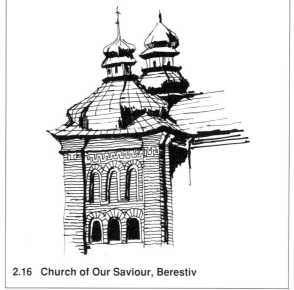

2.16 Church of Our Saviour, Berestiv

ornament. In the late seventeenth century, St. Sophia's was rebuilt with elaborate baroque-style pediments, and the windows were set in decorative surrounds typical of the architecture of that period [fig. 2.18]. This is the way it still stands.

In the twelfth century, as the Kievan State broke up into smaller principalities, financial resources became less abundant, and churches were built on a more modest scale. Concurrently, their architectural ornamentation changed, consisting mainly of frescoes, carved stone and majolica³ plates. Construction became simpler and more compact, though quite distinctive in style [fig. 2.19].

An important stylistic development of the twelfth and thirteenth centuries was that

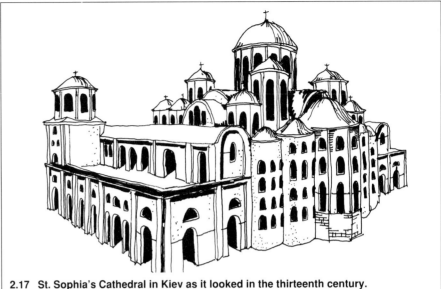

2.17 St. Sophia's Cathedral in Kiev as it looked in the thirteenth century.

of the onion dome [fig. 2.20], which is believed to have originated in the northern parts of Rus', possibly the Novgorod region. Two conditions prevailed there: the traditional building material was wood rather than stone, and the region had heavy snowfalls. The Byzantine dome underwent some dramatic changes. In order to accommodate the structural stresses characteristic of wood-frame construction, the members were tied around the bottom and slightly pinched. A peak was added to the dome to prevent the accumulation of snow. Though utilitarian in origin, the onion dome became a popular decorative motif that soon spread across the Kievan realm and consequently migrated south, where it became part of the architectural tradition. Thus there was an evolution of Ukrainian church styles from the Byzantine to the typical Kievan – which is a domed cruciform, or "cross-in-square" structure with a large onion dome at the centre, surrounded by four or more smaller domes.

26

2.18   St. Sophia's Cathedral as it looks now, showing the baroque renovation.

2.20   The onion dome made its appearance in the thirteenth century.

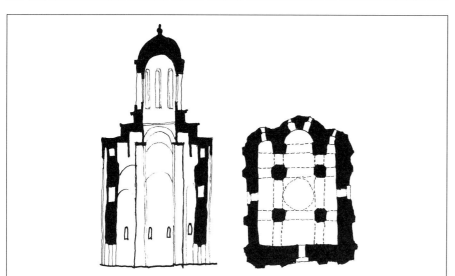

2.19   A typical church in the later Kievan architectural style. Note the cross-in-square configuration in plan.

27

WESTERN UKRAINIAN CHURCH ARCHITECTURE

When the state of Kievan Rus' disintegrated into several principalities under different dominant powers during the twelfth and thirteenth centuries, church architecture underwent further changes. In the West, especially after the Tatar invasion, Galicia became the leading centre of Rus'. Cities such as Halych, Peremyshl' and L'viv emerged. Each of these inherited the characteristic Byzantine church styles of Kiev. However, because of strong political links that began to develop in the mid-twelfth century with western European lands, architectural influences such as Romanesque [fig. 2.21], Gothic [fig. 2.22] and Renaissance [fig. 2.23] extended into Ukraine. As portions of Ukraine came first under the domination of Lithuanian princes, then of the Polish kings (during the fourteenth to eighteenth centuries), the people absorbed some western European influences, and various modifications to traditional church architecture appeared. Round churches were occasionally built in this period. For example, in the village of

2.21 Romanesque architecture was characterized by rounded vaults and arches.

2.22 Gothic architecture made use of technical advances that permitted a more dynamic distribution of stresses than the Romanesque; it was characterized by soaring and pointed volumes, vaults and arches.

Horiany near Uzhhorod, a church-rotunda with apses embedded in the walls appeared; there were similar churches in the village of Poberezhzhia near Halych, as well as in the Church of Volodymyr Volyns'kyi [fig. 2.24].

Occasionally, Romanesque elements made their appearance. The Romanesque style, found predominantly in Italy from the twelfth to the fourteenth centuries, was characterized by rounded arches and vaults.

2.23 Renaissance architecture was characterized by sober lines and the rhythmical use of sculptured decorative motifs.

2.24 The rotunda of the Church of Volodymyr Volyns'kyi: (a) plan, (b) section.

A fine example of Byzantino-Romanesque style is the relatively well-preserved Church of St. Panteleimon in Halych, built in the late twelfth century.

During the Tatar invasion and well into the sixteenth century, the unsettled political conditions of the land required that most churches be adapted to provide shelter and withstand sieges. The Church of St. Mary the Protectress in Sutkivtsi (1426) [fig. 2.25] is a good example. These churches had such defensive features as thick walls, loopholes, machiolate parapets and towers.

The Gothic style, which came in the wake of the Romanesque, exerted some influence on Ukrainian church architecture. It appeared around the fifteenth century, mostly coming from Silesia and Bohemia, and was particularly strong in the neighbouring areas. It never penetrated deeply into Ukrainian lands, where the influence was more subtle and indirect. It was characterized by twin-tower facades, pointed towers, portals and arches, star-shaped vaulting, counterbalancing buttresses, and upward-extended windows. Orthodox churches frequently retained the plans and dimensions established during the Kievan Rus' period (for example, in three-nave churches, the naves were the same height, and there were cupolas), but often in combination with some elements of the Gothic style. Examples of this can be found in Holy Trinity Church in Mezhyrich (built in the middle of the fifteenth century) [fig. 2.26].

Still another Western influence came from neighbouring Moldavia during the fifteenth and sixteenth centuries, where churches with three conchae (shells) were common. St. Onuphrius Church in Husiatyn [fig. 2.27] is a good example.

2.25 The fortified Church of St. Mary the Protectress, Sutkivtsi

UKRAINIAN BAROQUE CHURCH ARCHITECTURE

The establishment of the Cossack state in the seventeenth century fostered a resurgence of Ukrainian church architecture. In the process of state building, Ukrainians began to restore old churches and to build new ones. Also, economic circumstances allowed for new city and town churches. Wooden church architecture, however, continued to flourish during the seventeenth and eighteenth centuries in the rural areas. Even during the division of the Ukrainian Cossack state between Poland and Muscovy, this creative church building process continued. Under the enlightened leadership of certain hetmans[4], especially Ivan Mazepa, a program of restoration and construction of churches was undertaken, and, for the first time since the emergence of the "Kievan school" in the

30

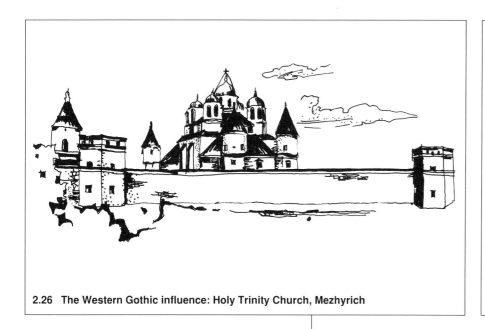

2.26   The Western Gothic influence: Holy Trinity Church, Mezhyrich

2.27   St. Onuphrius Church, Husiatyn. The conchae, or apse-like appendages at the side of the church, reflect a Western influence in ecclesiastical architecture.

twelfth century, a national style began to develop. According to architectural historian George Korbyn, "Ukrainian architecture [evolved into] an entirely different, dynamic and unique style, 'the Ukrainian Baroque,' a distinctly national Ukrainian style."[5] This style, sometimes referred to as "Cossack baroque," was characterized by an elaborate (at times excessive) ornamentation of buildings, the addition of purely decorative elements, and an emphasis on the facade. A particularly distinctive feature of this style was the treatment of the onion dome; it now had angular elements, was tiered, and had a protruding flashing at the base. The restored St. Sophia's Cathedral is an example of this architectural style. Other good examples exist in Chernihiv and Hlukhiv, which were important centres in the Cossack state.

RECENT UKRAINIAN CHURCH ARCHITECTURE

At the end of the eighteenth century, Ukraine was divided politically between the Russian and the Austro-Hungarian empires, both of which influenced church architecture. Within the Russian Empire, all church affairs were centralized under the Holy Synod, the ruling body of the Russian Church in St. Petersburg, and church construction in eastern Ukraine conformed to norms established by this body. Church construction in the provinces of Galicia and Bukovyna was influenced by western European architectural movements. Even so, and especially in the rural areas, church architecture faithfully retained its Byzantine-Ukrainian traits, and in some respects reached its peak of evolution in the eighteenth century. In the late nineteenth century, stone structures became more common, replacing the old wooden ones. These stone structures maintained traditions of earlier periods, occasionally showing traits adapted from western European architecture.

An entirely new phase of Ukrainian architecture emerged in the twentieth century. Church building was severely limited in western Ukraine under Poland between the two world wars; it has not been allowed in Ukrainian lands under communist regimes. Moreover, countless churches have been destroyed in both eastern and western Ukraine in the Soviet period. Thus, the development of the Ukrainian architectural tradition has been halted on its native soil. It flourishes only in those countries where Ukrainian immigrants have settled, such as Canada, the United States, Australia, Argentina, Brazil and western Europe.

THE STYLES OF UKRAINIAN CHURCH ARCHITECTURE

3

THE VAST TERRITORY OF UKRAINE is made up of many geographical regions which, throughout history, were influenced by many cultural currents, and which developed their own regional identities. As a result, a great diversity of church styles is found there [fig. 3.1]. The Christianization of Kievan Rus' marked the beginning of the construction of great churches on the Byzantine model. Gradually, under the influence of the creative genius of indigenous builders and, later, in response to western European and other architectural trends, an evolution of Ukrainian church building took place. However, this evolution was not uniform. Generally speaking, city churches retained a more pronounced Byzantine style, which is apparent to this day, while rural churches evolved with a variety of forms and decorations that relied on wood. The mountain regions of western Ukraine were particularly well suited to the development of a rich tradition of wooden architectural styles. In the rural areas of the plains regions, stone churches gained favour during the eighteenth and nineteenth centuries.[1]

KIEVAN STYLE

The architectural style designated here as Kievan prevails in the region of Ukraine centred in Kiev, encompassing the central and eastern plains.

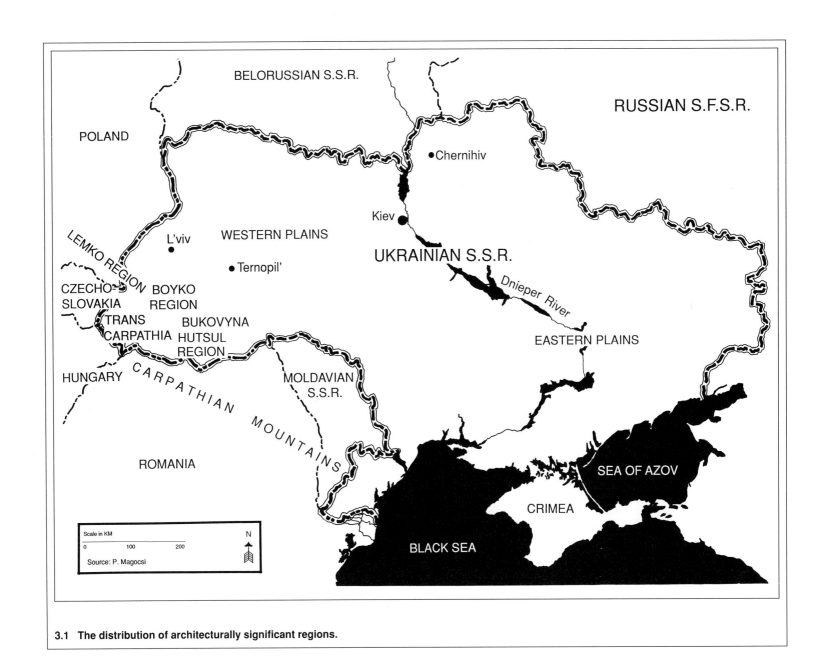

BELORUSSIAN S.S.R.

RUSSIAN S.F.S.R.

POLAND

●Chernihiv

Kiev ●

LEMKO REGION

L'viv ●

WESTERN PLAINS

UKRAINIAN S.S.R.

● Ternopil'

CZECHO-
SLOVAKIA

BOYKO
REGION

Dnieper River

TRANS
CARPATHIA

BUKOVYNA

HUTSUL
REGION

EASTERN PLAINS

HUNGARY

C A R P A T H I A N

MOLDAVIAN
S.S.R.

M O U N T A I N S

ROMANIA

SEA OF AZOV

CRIMEA

Scale in KM

0   100   200

N

BLACK SEA

Source: P. Magocsi

3.1   The distribution of architecturally significant regions.

34

A variety of layouts ranging from the basilica to a cruciform floor plan can be found in Kievan architecture as it evolved over a period of ten centuries. The Kievan style is characterized primarily by its rich superstructure, which may vary from the austere to the exuberant, and the grandeur of its interior spaces (see illustrations in chapter 2). The best example of the Kievan style is the St. Sophia Cathedral in Kiev. The style has evolved in response to technological and cultural changes, but has always maintained its essence and its basic silhouette. The Kievan style, being the style of the historic capital of Ukraine, has served as a cultural beacon, and has consistently been an inspiration for other Ukrainian regional styles.

WESTERN UKRAINIAN MOUNTAIN STYLE

Western Ukraine, which in the nineteenth century consisted of Galicia, Bukovyna and sub-Carpathian Rus', where most nineteenth-century immigrants to Manitoba originated, is the principal homeland of Ukrainian styles and techniques of log-and-timber construction. This area reaches from the southeastern corner of present-day Poland to the Romanian border, the western tip of which is, to this day, part of Czechoslovakia. In the course of history, western Ukraine continually found itself being divided, subdivided and dominated by its more powerful neighbours. As a result, local populations developed a strong sense of local identity as well as distinct architectural styles, though over the centuries, they remained faithful to their Byzantine religious architectural tradition, which provided a certain uniformity among styles.

The people in the wooded Carpathian mountain regions lived mainly in villages, and the construction of a church was a community enterprise. The village would retain the services of a master carpenter or architect (usually one and the same person) who would discuss the church's design with the villagers at great length, and then employ a

35

team of carpenters. The timber for the church had to be cut in the spring, before the rising of the sap, and left to season until the following winter. During the winter the timber would be moved to the site, and construction would begin in the spring, a year after the timber was cut. A church could take up to four years to build, due to problems inherent in working with wood, for example, the process of curing the timber and larger structural members.

The foundations were usually light, suggesting that the churches were not intended to last a long time. Sometimes large stones were used at the corners and other strategic points, and upon these a level rectangular foundation of timbers was laid at varying heights above the uneven ground. These timbers were comparatively massive, typically up to 45 by 35 centimetres in cross-sectional dimension, and as long as twelve metres.

The walls were constructed so that timbers would protrude near the top to form cantilevered brackets, or consoles; these served to support the eaves, which often overhung, forming the roof of an external gallery [fig. 3.3]. This unique system of roof support, based on the inherent resistance of wood to bending stresses, found particular favour with the Boyko and other peoples of the eastern Carpathians.

In the more western parts of the Carpathian regions, a different architectural evolution was taking place. As early as the sixteenth century, the techniques of timber framing and raftering of roofs and towers were advancing from western Europe. The Poles were quick to pick up such changes and adopted the raftered roof. They also began timber framing, as did the Lemko. However, these innovations were primarily restricted to general construction,

3.2 *Opasannia* is the Ukrainian term for the gallery around the perimeter of the church; it is formed by a continuous overhang.

3.3 Log construction detail showing supported roof overhang.

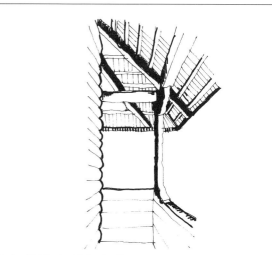

3.4 *Piddashshia* is the Ukrainian term for eaves, or overhang. The *piddashshia* may be supported by brackets or columns.

whereas churches retained the more traditional technique of timber laying.[2]

An architectural form peculiar to many Carpathian wooden churches is the external covered gallery known in Ukrainian as *opasannia* [fig. 3.2]. The galleries themselves were formed by structural overhangs known as *piddashshia*, or *piddashok* [fig. 3.4]; the overhangs consisted of extended eaves supported by brackets made of projecting wall timbers or upright posts. These galleries served to protect the external walls, and any parishioners who might be there, from the weather. They were built primarily in the Lemko and Boyko regions.

Lemko Region
The Lemko region is in the southwest corner of western Ukraine, in the westernmost part of the Carpathian region. The Lemko people built their churches according to a three-chamber plan [fig. 3.5]. Typically it had three towers, one over each section of the church, each being slightly lower than the other, the tallest one in the west. The nave and sanctuary were usually constructed of logs laid horizontally, while the main, or western, tower was usually framed. In the central and eastern parts of the Lemko region, the frame structure was mounted on the horizontal beams of the narthex ceiling. The western tower, which

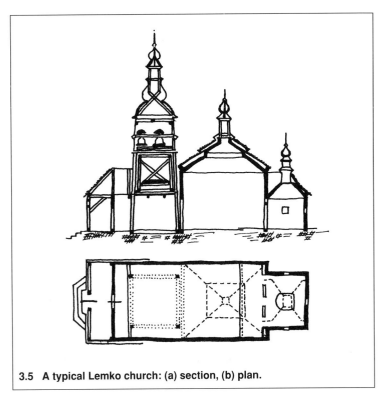

3.5 A typical Lemko church: (a) section, (b) plan.

3.6 The Gothic influence in a Lemko church is evident in the treatment of the turrets and spire.

3.7 On occasion, Lemko churches were covered with a single, high, gable roof, exemplified by this eighteenth-century church in Dibrova. The interior normally retained its three-chamber configuration.

dominated the structure in height, housed the belfry, and was influenced by western European and Polish traditions. As well, Gothic turrets and spires were occasionally used as decorative motifs [fig. 3.6], in all likelihood brought to the Carpathian mountain regions by German immigrants in the eighteenth century.

There are Lemko churches that had only one tower (equivalent to the western tower in the three-tower church); the nave and sanctuary in the one-tower church were covered by a high gable roof [fig. 3.7]; the sanctuary was always smaller in area than the nave, and could be located in a rectangular or polygonal apse. The light in the nave was usually admitted by small windows. The preferred building materials were oak and ash. Both *opasannia* and *piddashshia* are found in Lemko churches.

Boyko Region

The Boyko region lies just southeast of the Lemko region. The Boyko people by and large resisted outside influences and remained faithful to the old log, or blockwork, technique (believed by some authorities to be the common legacy of the Slavs). Boyko churches were built on a three-chamber plan, following ancient Byzantine tradition, with the tallest tower at the centre; this feature distinguishes the Boyko from the Lemko churches [fig. 3.8]. Also, the central area, or nave, is broader than the narthex or sanctuary. Boyko churches generally had square sanctuaries instead of apsidal ones.

The preferred building materials for Boyko churches were, as for the Lemko churches, oak and ash. Both *opas-annia* and *piddashshia* were present but, un-like the Lemko churches, the Boyko churches had bell towers that were separate structures, isolated from the building itself.

An interesting feature of certain Boyko churches was the alternation of vertical and successively receding sloping sections in the roofs, creating a unique tiered effect. An example of a Boyko church of this type can be found at the Architectural Museum in L'viv [fig. 3.9].

In Boyko churches the walls were built of heavy horizontal timbers jointed at the corners; there was no framed timber, no raftering of roofs. Owing to the perishable nature of wood, it is not surprising that few wooden churches built prior to the seventeenth century exist.

Hutsul Region

The Hutsul region lies to the east of the Boyko region, along the headwaters of the Tisa River. The distinctive features of Hutsul churches are their particular roofline and floor plan [fig. 3.10]. Hutsul churches were nearly always built according to the cruciform plan, with five sections instead of the three more commonly found in the Carpathian churches. Some researchers attribute this anomaly to the fact that the Hutsul people were at one time more prosperous than their neighbours and could afford the more complex plan, and that their settlements were more concentrated. As a result, fewer but bigger churches were built.

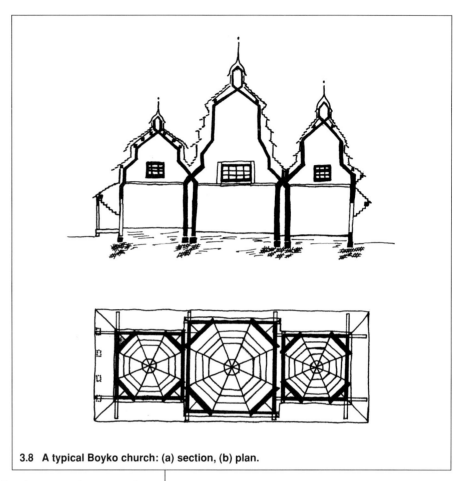

3.8 A typical Boyko church: (a) section, (b) plan.

40

The roofing over the central section consisted of an octahedral drum placed over the squared section, on top of which was placed a "tent frame," or octagonal pyramid. The roofs over the remaining four arms were doubly sloped, with a gable at each end. The roof was supported by brackets built up from the projecting wall timbers. Like the Boyko churches, Hutsul churches had *opasannia*. The most common building material was spruce, which the Hutsul axed longitudinally into semi-logs and placed with their round sides up.

3.9 **More affluent Boyko communities favoured an exuberant multi-tiered design. This church is part of the Boyko exhibit at the Architectural Museum in L'viv.**

The Bukovynian Region

The Bukovynian region lies to the east of the Hutsul region and borders on Romania. The Bukovynian church is a simple rectangular structure with a gable roof [fig. 3.11]. However, the east end of the structure, where the sanctuary is located, ends in a polygonal form. The west end of the structure, where the entrance is located, is either flat or polygonal. Thus, the Bukovynian church can be polygonal or nearly elliptical. In the elliptical plan the ends of the roof may be dramatically splayed to follow the polygonal shape. Occasionally the roofs feature *opasannia*, supported by vertically carved rafters. Typically the roof shingles were carved from wood. Bukovynian churches were usually built of logs, sometimes stuccoed with clay and whitewashed on the exterior.

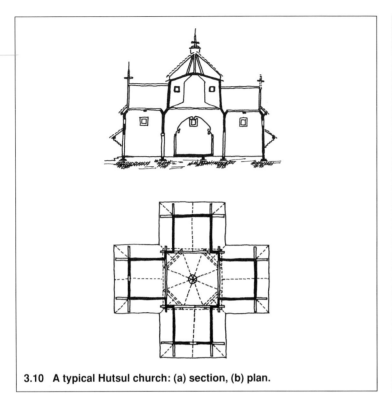

3.10 A typical Hutsul church: (a) section, (b) plan.

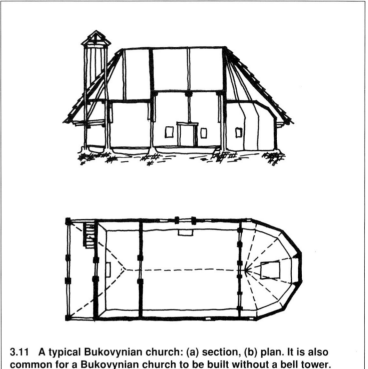

3.11 A typical Bukovynian church: (a) section, (b) plan. It is also common for a Bukovynian church to be built without a bell tower.

WESTERN UKRAINIAN PLAINS STYLE, TERNOPIL' REGION

Two distinct architectural styles developed in the plateau region located between the eastern plains of Ukraine and the Carpathian mountains, north of Bukovyna and the Hutsul region. The Ternopil' district is its centre, and it is where the greatest number of churches built in these styles is found. The Ternopil' district was surrounded by various regions displaying very strong architectural traditions, and the two architectural styles that developed are a blend of a number of these traditions, particularly Kievan and Carpathian. Although churches of

42

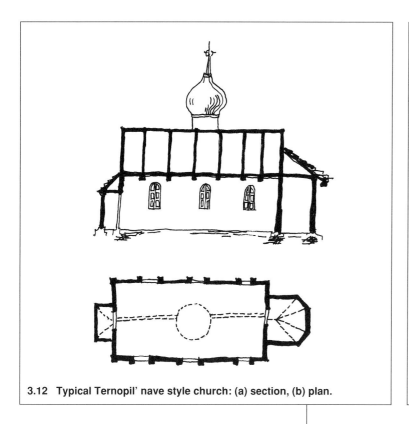

3.12 Typical Ternopil' nave style church: (a) section, (b) plan.

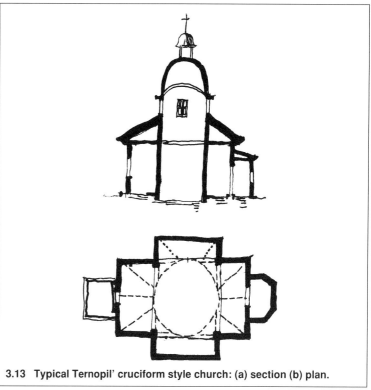

3.13 Typical Ternopil' cruciform style church: (a) section (b) plan.

the Ternopil' style have occasionally been built of wood, a greater number of examples exist in stone, especially in urban areas. Stone from the natural quarries in the many river canyons that cut through the plateau was readily available for church construction.

Ternopil' Nave Style

The Ternopil' nave church bears a certain resemblance to the Bukovynian church. It is a single structure with an iconostasis separating the sanctuary from the nave. However, this style differs from the Bukovynian style in that it lacks the polygonal shape in the sanctuary, and the

43

roof is gabled rather than splayed at the ends. In addition, there is a small decorative dome in the middle of the roof [fig. 3.12].

In the seventeenth century there was a trend towards increasing the size of the central decorative dome in a fashion reminiscent of the Boyko churches, and making it structurally a part of the roof so that the dome's interior could be seen from inside the nave. Unlike the churches in the Boyko region, the Ternopil' nave churches retained the gable roofing on the east and west ends.

Ternopil' Cruciform Style
The Ternopil' cruciform style appears to be a combination of the Hutsul and the Ternopil' nave styles [fig. 3.13]. Churches of this style have a cruciform plan with all the arms of the cross of equal length. The roofing over the nave, apse and transepts is gabled, and has a dome over the central section. This dome is not decorative, but structural, and can be seen from the inside. It is what distinguishes the Ternopil' cruciform church from the Hutsul church. Churches of this style were often built of masonry in urban areas.

TRADITIONAL CHURCH ARCHITECTURE IN MANITOBA

4

MOST OF THE TRADITIONAL CHURCH STYLES that evolved in Ukraine from the eleventh through nineteenth centuries are represented in Manitoba. However, because of the marked differences in the conditions the new immigrants and their descendants encountered in Manitoba, few of the churches were built in a purely traditional style. Two strong forces have influenced the evolution of church design in Manitoba: tradition and pragmatism. Traditional images of the homeland originals were fresh in people's minds, and there was an emotional tendency to reproduce the familiar. However, the relative poverty of the early settlers, the cost of building materials, and the attraction of better Canadian construction methods called for change.

KIEVAN STYLE

Most of the Ukrainian people who settled in Manitoba came from Galicia and other parts of western Ukraine. It is interesting to note, however, that they tended to use old Kievan models as a standard for national expression when they began building their churches in Manitoba. Churches of the Kievan style are characterized by their rich architectural detail. Although the floor plans were generally cruciform, there were variations; the common features, however, were the great domes and majestic interior spaces. The domes, oftentimes two-tiered, were typically placed on rather tall drums, a feature that gave the Kievan church its distinctive look [fig. 4.1]. The actual shape of the domes depended on the historical model upon which a particular church had been based. Although there are no churches in Manitoba that are absolutely true to the Kievan style, three examples are near to it, and illustrate some particular aspect.

Ukrainian Catholic Church of the Resurrection, Dauphin

The Church of the Resurrection [fig. 4.2] exemplifies the early Kievan style in its cruciform plan, the treatment of the domes and towers, the overall proportions of the structure, and the manner in which the elements of the building are distributed. The interior spaces of the church provide the viewer with the nearest possible experience of a traditional Kievan church.

4.1 KIEVAN STYLE
St. Sophia's Cathedral in Kiev, shown here as it looked in the thirteenth century, is the prototype of the Kievan architectural style.

The Church of the Resurrection, built in 1936, was designed by Fr. Philip Ruh. Mike Yanchynsky, who assisted Fr. Ruh in the construction of many churches, was the head carpenter. The church site includes a bell tower, a cross, a rectory and a hall. Fr. Andrew Roborets'ky served the parish at the time of the construction.

This unique building has become a well-known landmark in the Dauphin landscape. It belongs to the group of four remarkable churches sometimes called "Fr. Ruh's prairie cathedrals." Two of them have disappeared; the Dauphin church and the Immaculate Conception Ukrainian Catholic Church at Cooks Creek remain as the only examples in Manitoba of Ruh's work in this style. The product of Depression volunteer labour, it was completed before the Second World War, and since then has defined the town as the home of many Ukrainian Canadians.

St. Mary the Protectress Ukrainian Orthodox Cathedral, Winnipeg

The Cathedral of St. Mary the Protectress[1] [fig. 4.3] is the best example in Manitoba of a Kievan church executed in the Ukrainian baroque style, particularly in the design of its domes. The richly executed iconostasis is also a fine example of traditional iconography. The frescoes hint at the magnificent decoration of old Kievan churches, the walls of which were completely covered with icons.

The two towers, because they are located in the facade, are not a truly traditional feature, but are characteristic of the Gothic influence, which came to be an accepted pattern in Manitoba (see chapter 5).

The parish was founded in 1924 and held its first liturgies in a nearby Anglican church. In 1925 ten lots were purchased for $2,600, on Sinclair Avenue between Burrows and Magnus in Winnipeg. Stephan Meush was the architect, general contractor and designer of the iconostasis. Construction began in July 1925, and services were held in the basement until the upper level was completed in 1951. The church was constructed over the years mostly by an energetic volunteer labour force. The interior iconography was done by Sviatoslav Hordynsky.

Transfiguration Ukrainian Orthodox Church, Pine River

Although small, the Church of the Transfiguration [fig. 4.4] is a good example of the Kievan architectural style. It embodies few baroque elements, and these are mostly expressed in the ridged appearance of the domes, and in the lantern supporting the smaller central dome. The distribution of the volumes and the location of the four secondary

4.3 The Cathedral of St. Mary the Protectress in Winnipeg is a good example of Ukrainian baroque ornamentation.

4.2 Among the churches in Manitoba, the Church of the Resurrection in Dauphin seems to have captured best the feel of Kievan interior spaces.

4.4   The Church of the Transfiguration, Pine River

domes is particularly Kievan in spirit. The mass of gilded domes makes this church an impressive sight in the expanse of the prairies. The two smaller domes on either side of the entrance are attributable to a Gothic influence.

Fr. C. Hrebeniuk, a priest of the Russian Orthodox Mission, established this parish in 1926, and the church was built in 1929.

WESTERN UKRAINIAN MOUNTAIN STYLE

The largest segment of Manitobans of Ukrainian descent traces its origins to Galicia, Bukovyna and the Carpathian mountain regions, where timber was the principal building material, and where distinctive architectural styles developed. The architectural styles of these regions are well represented in Manitoba, but, because of the lack of appropriate building materials, they were most affected by the process of adaptation to Canadian conditions. The churches built in Manitoba retained their traditional silhouette, but the striking texture, especially of the Lemko and Boyko styles, could not be easily replicated in Manitoba. The example that is most representative of several features of traditional Carpathian wooden architecture is the St. Volodymyr Chapel at Camp Morton.

St. Volodymyr Ukrainian Catholic Chapel, Camp Morton

The St. Volodymyr Chapel [fig. 4.5] was built with the help of skilled workers brought to Manitoba for the express purpose of demonstrating the craft of traditional church building to young Manitobans of Ukrainian descent. In plan, the church is rather simple and func-

4.5 St. Volodymyr Chapel in Camp Morton was built as a demonstration of Carpathian regional skill.

4.6   The St. Volodymyr Chapel has a covered gallery known as an *opasannia*.

tional, and doesn't reflect one particular regional style. The central dome, with its "tent-frame" roof, is of Hutsul style. The log-and-timber construction embodies all the traditional building techniques of that style: it has a carefully executed exterior gallery (see chapter 3); and, the logs at the corner joints are cantilevered in a typical manner to provide support for the overhang [fig. 4.6]. The interior framing is modelled after Carpathian structures as well. By putting the chapel in a thickly wooded area, the designer successfully created a setting reminiscent of a Carpathian mountain valley.

The building of the chapel was commissioned by the Ukrainian Catholic Archdiocese of Canada to serve the religious needs of a summer camp for three Ukrainian Catholic youth organizations of Manitoba (Ukrainian Catholic Youth, Plast, and the Ukrainian Youth Association of Canada). Fr. Joseph Denischuk supervised the project, Roman Kowch from Detroit designed the structure, while Mr. Pidstawka from Fisher Branch was master builder. Construction was completed in 1962. The cost of the iconostasis, carved in wood by George Buchynsky, was underwritten by the Blessed Virgin Mary Parish of Winnipeg. The metropolitan of the Ukrainian Catholic Church, Maxim Hermaniuk, donated an icon of the Blessed Virgin Mary painted by Roman Kowal.

Lemko Style
Lemko churches are characterized by a three-chambered plan, the largest chamber being the central one. The most distinctive feature of the Lemko style is the presence of three towers; the tallest tower is located at the front of the church, a broader and shorter one is over the

centre, and the third and smallest is over the sanctuary [fig. 4.7]. Some Lemko churches have only the front tower, the rest of the church being covered by a single massive, steep roof.

Few Lemko people immigrated to western Canada, and churches resembling the Lemko style in Manitoba cannot be entirely attributed to an emigratrion from that area.

Holy Resurrection Orthodox Church, Sifton

The distribution of volumes in the Church of the Holy Resurrection is typically Lemko [fig. 4.8]. It has a three-chambered plan and three domes arranged in descending order. The first dome is mounted on a tall tower at the front of the church, a larger but lower dome covers the central chamber, and the smallest and lowest dome is set over the sanctuary. However, architectural details and decorative treatments are a combination of a number of other regional styles, mostly Kievan.

The church was built in 1928 under the auspices of the Russian Orthodox Mission. It is currently under the jurisdiction of the Orthodox Church of America.

4.7 LEMKO STYLE
The typical Lemko church is three chambered, the tallest tower at the front.

Holy Trinity Ukrainian Orthodox Church, Valley River

The Holy Trinity Church [fig. 4.9] has a characteristic three-chambered plan, and it diminishes in height from narthex to sanctuary; the sanctuary, however, is surmounted by a cross rather than by a smaller tower. It was originally a Russian Orthodox mission church, a fact that is reflected in some aspects of its architecture.

4.8 Church of the Holy Resurrection, Sifton

4.9   Holy Trinity Church, Valley River

4.10   Church of the Nativity of the Blessed Virgin Mary, Rembrandt

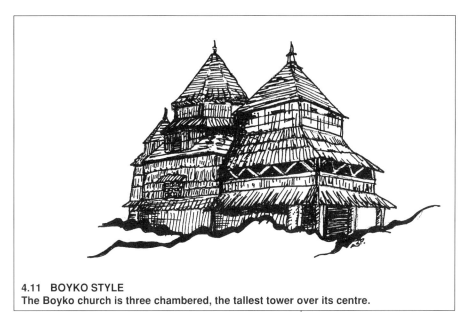

4.11 BOYKO STYLE
The Boyko church is three chambered, the tallest tower over its centre.

Ukrainian Catholic Church of the Nativity of the Blessed Virgin Mary, Rembrandt

The Church of the Nativity of the Blessed Virgin Mary [fig. 4.10], although possessing only two elements of the traditional Lemko style, nevertheless conveys its spirit. The decorative treatment of the tower and the corner gables suggests a Gothic variation of the Lemko style (the typical spire-and-four-turrets configuration), as does the steep roof covering the entire church. A porch replaces the front chamber of the traditional plan and, in a way, suggests an *opasannia*.

The church was built in 1917 one mile from the town of Rembrandt. It cost the parish $600 to purchase the four-acre lot and to build the church. A cemetery and a bell tower are located on the church property. The Order of Redemptorist Fathers (CSSR), which had a chapter house in Komarno at that time, supplied the parish with priests between 1916 and 1923.

Boyko Style
The basic plan of Boyko churches has three chambers, the largest in the centre. Each of these is surmounted by a tower, the tallest and largest of which is built over the large central chamber [fig. 4.11].

Many Manitoba Ukrainian churches were built in the Boyko style. However, as is the case with most wooden churches built here in the mountain style, the Boyko churches of Manitoba exhibit neither the typical timber-construction framework nor the rich texture and craftwork of the Carpathian mountain churches. However, they do possess a number of features that identify them as Boyko: a three-chambered plan, the overall distribution of volumes, and, sometimes, the hint of a tiered tower.

St. Michael's Ukrainian Orthodox Church, Gardenton

St. Michael's Church in Gardenton [fig. 4.12], built in 1899, is the oldest Ukrainian church in Manitoba, and replicates the homeland tradition in a number of ways. It was built according to the three-chambered plan, the central part of the structure being the largest. It was a log structure built mainly of natural local materials, and it was erected using elementary methods, a fact that is of particular interest to the architectural historian.

The original Boyko appearance was masked in 1901 by the addition of wood siding and the replacement of the thatched roof by shingles. The addition of tin-covered cupolas further altered the appearance of the church.

Wasyl Kykot headed the construction of the church with the aid of forty-four volunteer builders whose names are listed in a document formally sealed in the altar. The parish committee, formed in 1897, had negotiated a special grant with the Dominion Government for twenty acres, which was issued on 25 May 1899. After considerable deliberation among the parishioners, a site was chosen on the south side of the Roseau River. The parishioners began using the land immediately for a cemetery; its oldest cross is dated 1899 and is believed to be that of an immigrant child. The first liturgy was celebrated in October 1899 and Fr. Constantine Popoff, a Russian Orthodox missionary priest, officiated.[2]

St. Michael's Church was designated an historic site, the first Ukrainian church in Manitoba to receive this honour.[3]

4.12 St. Michael's Church, Gardenton

St. Nicholas Ukrainian Catholic Church, Poplarfield

St. Nicholas Church [fig. 4.13] is a modest church that possesses characteristics of a Boyko church: it is a three-chambered structure, and the central cell, being the tallest part of the building, is extended upwards into a dome. The distribution of volumes is striking and, although the church is built of standard materials, it illustrates well the traditional Boyko style.

St. Nicholas Church is situated on a one-acre plot in the town of Poplarfield. It was built in 1913 at a cost of $3,000. The Redemptorist Fathers from Komarno served the parish in the early years. The iconography and interior artwork was done by Jacob Maydanyk. The bell tower stands next to the church, and the cemetery is located half a mile away.

St. Michael's Ukrainian Catholic Church, Mink Creek

St. Michael's Church in Mink Creek [fig. 4.14] is also three-chambered, its central chamber being the tallest and largest. The hip roof and Romanesque windows are not traditional, however, having been built according to local practices. The bell tower is traditional, embodying many elements of western Ukrainian wooden architecture.

The parishioners of the Mink Creek Parish considered themselves fortunate to have had Rev. Nestor Dmytriw, who had celebrated the first Ukrainian Catholic liturgy in Canada in April 1897, bless the site on which the church would be built.

Hutsul Style

The two main characteristics of a Hutsul church are the cruciform plan and an octagonal drum over the central portion, which is covered by a tent-frame roof [fig. 4.15]. A great many Ukrainian churches in Manitoba exhibit one or more of these characteristics. None of the existing churches, however, is made of logs. Of all the wooden churches in Ukraine, the Hutsul church style was probably the easiest one to

57

4.13 St. Nicholas Church, Poplarfield

4.14 St. Michael's Church, Mink Creek

4.15 HUTSUL STYLE
The typical Hutsul church is characterized by the octagonal tent-frame roof at its centre, as shown in this eighteenth-century church in Yasynia. Note the typical small domes at the gables.

replicate under Manitoba conditions because of the simplicity of its architecture. Many of the pioneer churches were built in a fairly traditional Hutsul style, but very few of them remain, especially in their original condition. A common feature of the Hutsul style churches in Manitoba is the elongation of the nave, or "western" arm of the cross, in a cruciform plan to accommodate the pews; this was a non-traditional addition to churches of the Byzantine rite.

Manitoba churches built in the Hutsul style are built of commercially available materials and lack the traditional wide overhanging *opasannia* and *piddashshia*.

Holy Trinity Ukrainian Catholic Church, Stuartburn

Holy Trinity Church [fig. 4.16] is a frame building that, with its cruciform plan and octagonal tent-frame roof, is a good example of the traditional Hutsul style. The small tower with its dome, and the little onion domes on the gables, are frequently found on Hutsul churches of the eighteenth and nineteenth centuries. The Gothic windows are a local variation that can be attributed to the kind of stock available at the local lumberyard.

Holy Trinity Church was built in 1902, but fire destroyed it, and a second very similar structure was built in 1911. The church is situated five miles west of Vita on a section of land donated by Michael Dumansky. Dumansky was also head carpenter. The bell tower, adjacent to the church, contains four bells.

Holy Transfiguration Independent Greek Church, Winnipeg

Holy Transfiguration Church [fig. 4.17] has the typical cruciform plan and an octagonal tent-frame roof over the dome. The church has lost some of the more pronounced characteristics of the Hutsul style; early photographs show that a decorative baroque bulb surmounted the dome, a feature of some nineteenth-century Hutsul churches.

The church was built in 1907 by the Consistory of the Independent

4.16 Holy Trinity Church, Stuartburn

Ruthenian Greek-Orthodox Church of Canada (commonly known as the Independent Greek Church). The congregation was later absorbed into the Presbyterian Church and, for theological reasons, the building was stripped of much of its traditional appearance. In the late 1930s, it was acquired by the Seventh Day Adventists, and in the mid-1980s it became a native evangelical centre – the Bethel Chapel for Indians and Metis.

4.17 Former Holy Transfiguration Independent Greek Church, Winnipeg

Sacred Heart Ukrainian Catholic Church, Tolstoi

Sacred Heart Church [fig. 4.18] has the typical cruciform plan, though the western arm is somewhat elongated to increase the length of the nave. The tent-frame octagonal roof is covered with sheet metal – a sign of modernization. In keeping with the Hutsul custom, sphere-mounted crosses have been placed on the east and west gables. The church was more true to the Hutsul model before it was covered with new siding.

The present church, built in 1928, replaced an earlier building erected in 1911, which was destroyed by fire in 1927. The interior was decorated by B. Kohut. Materials for the altars and the basic liturgical inventory were obtained at a cost of $1,500. There is a bell tower on the grounds, and the cemetery is located four kilometres from the church.

Holy Trinity Ukrainian Orthodox Church, Poplarfield

Holy Trinity Church [fig. 4.19], although built later than most Manitoba churches of this type, conforms to the Hutsul style: it has a cruciform plan with arms of equal length and an octagonal tent-frame roof. The treatment of the roof and the dome suggests the influence of the baroque and Ternopil' cruciform styles.

4.18 Sacred Heart Church, Tolstoi

4.19 Holy Trinity Church, Poplarfield

The parish was founded in 1944 and the church was built shortly afterwards by Michael Zuk.

Bukovynian Style

The Bukovynian church is typically a simple structure with a high-pitched roof; the sanctuary end of the structure, and sometimes the entrance as well, is semi-circular or polygonal. The eaves are usually supported by carved cantilevered rafters [fig. 4.20]. There are two excellent examples of Bukovynian church architecture in Manitoba, one in Lennard, and the other in Sirko.

St. Elie Romanian/Ukrainian Orthodox Church, Lennard

Recently restored, St. Elie Church [fig. 4.21], built of square-hewn logs, is a very good example of traditional timber construction. The interior of the church has been restored to its original appearance and contains artifacts that pioneers had brought from their home-land. All the elements of the building that had deteriorated were replaced with re-created hand-crafted materials. The eaves supports are lovingly carved and decorated.

This church was built in 1908 by Romanian and Ukrainian pioneers from Bukovyna. It replaced an earlier structure built of sod and logs in 1903. Alexie Slusarchuk designed the 1908 church, which was built on land donated by Elie Burla. John Paulenko later donated an additional two acres. The banners, crosses, icons and other church relics were brought

4.20 Holy Trinity Church in Chernivtsi is a typical Bukovynian church; it is rather small, with one roof covering all the chambers.

64

4.21 St. Elie Church, Lennard

from the homeland by the pioneers. This church served the parishioners until 1952, when a bigger church was erected to meet the needs of the growing community. The 1908 structure was restored in the 1970s and officially dedicated as an historic site in 1974, the seventy-fifth anniversary of the founding of the parish.[4]

St. Elias Ukrainian Orthodox Church, Sirko
St. Elias Church [fig. 4.22] was built according to a method of construction very similar to that used for the St. Elie Church in Lennard. Both were constructed about the same time, utilizing, for the most part, techniques the pioneers brought with them from their homeland. The high-pitched roof extends on exterior brackets, suggesting the traditional *opasannia*. The bell tower, constructed in the traditional western Ukrainian timber-construction style, is of particular interest.

Built in 1909, St. Elias Church was designed by Manoly Khalaturnyk. The original iconostasis is still in place. The church was recently restored and dedicated by the community as an historic site. The church site includes a bell tower and cemetery, as well as a new church constructed in 1950 to serve the present needs of the parish.

WESTERN UKRAINIAN PLAINS STYLE

Most of the Ukrainians who migrated to Canada at the turn of the century came from the region of Ternopil', in western Ukraine. It is therefore understandable that so many churches in Manitoba were built in the style of that region. Both the Ternopil' nave style and the Ternopil' cruciform style are well represented in Manitoba.

65

Ternopil' Nave Style

The Ternopil' nave style embodies essentially a plain rectangular structure with a gable roof, surmounted by a small dome in the centre, usually of baroque design, and a gable-roofed sanctuary, somewhat smaller than the nave [fig. 4.23]. Because of the simplicity of its design, churches of this style are found in great numbers in Manitoba.

4.22 St. Elias Church, Sirko

Assumption of the Blessed Virgin Mary Ukrainian Catholic Church, Ashville

The Assumption of the Blessed Virgin Mary Church [fig. 4.24] stands alone, surrounded by fields and scrub poplar. The pioneers who built it were still very close to the homeland building tradition, and this church is a close replica of a small country church in the Ternopil' region. The church is still very much like it was in the early years, without electricity, and heated by a wood stove.

The church was constructed in 1906. The two acres on which the church stands were donated by Peter Gara. There are neither iconostasis nor wall murals inside. An iconostasis once existed, but it was removed after a shift in the foundation. A bell tower, containing one bell, has been constructed, mostly from local materials, in a small bluff nearby. The cemetery is situated apart from the church, on two acres of land donated by O. Yakymyshyn.

St. Demetrius Ukrainian Orthodox Church, Camp Veselka

In its original location in Malonton, St. Demetrius Church [fig. 4.25] was set in a clump of spruce trees, surrounded by pasture. It is a very simple structure. The design of its interior space and the furnishings was

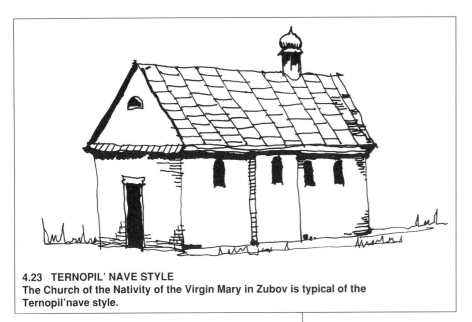

4.23 TERNOPIL' NAVE STYLE
The Church of the Nativity of the Virgin Mary in Zubov is typical of the
Ternopil'nave style.

4.24 Assumption of the Blessed Virgin Mary Church, Ashville

4.26 St. Demetrius Church as it looks now, after the move to Camp Veselka near Gimli.

4.25 St. Demetrius Church; view of the church in its original site at Malonton.

influenced by a variety of factors. The economic deprivation of the congregation that built it was reflected in the artifacts found in the church. For example, many articles were hand-crafted from everyday objects, and the pews were old movie-theatre seats. The church had no electricity and was heated by a wood stove. It has been moved to Camp Veselka near Gimli where, fully refurbished, it is used for worship by summer campers and other visitors [fig. 4.26].

Ternopil' Cruciform Style
The distinctive feature of the Ternopil' cruciform style is the massive dome that dominates the structure [fig. 4.27]. In Manitoba, the often-octagonal shape of the dome suggests the Hutsul style, while the basic decorative motifs point decisively to the Kievan style. Several good examples of the Ternopil' cruciform style exist in Manitoba.

Sts. Peter and Paul Ukrainian Catholic Church, Clover Leaf

Of all of the churches designed by Fr. Ruh, the Sts. Peter and Paul Church in Clover Leaf is the one that most faithfully reflects the Ternopil' cruciform style without introducing culturally inappropriate elements [fig. 4.28]. The decorative elements show the preference Fr. Ruh had for the Kievan style during the 1940s and 1950s.

The Sts. Peter and Paul Church was built in 1943 from materials taken from the dismantled log Church of St. John the Baptist at Cooks Creek, originally erected in 1906. It was de-

4.27 TERNOPIL' CRUCIFORM STYLE
St. Nicholas Church in Terebovlia illustrates the Ternopil' cruciform style.

4.28   Sts. Peter and Paul Church, Clover Leaf

4.29 Sts. Peter and Paul Church, Glenella, ca. 1950; view of the original 1919 design.

4.30 Sts. Peter and Paul Church, Glenella, 1989, after renovations.

signed by Fr. Ruh and built under his personal supervision with the help of master carpenter N. Kowalyk. Parishioners provided the volunteer labour. The parish was very poor, and Fr. Ruh donated both time and money to see the church completed.

Sts. Peter and Paul Ukrainian Catholic Church, Glenella

Sts. Peter and Paul Church in Glenella [figs. 4.29 and 4.30] illustrates the way the traditional appearance of a church is lost in the process of renovation. It is a church of rather modest proportions built in the Ternopil' cruciform style. The decorative treatment of the domes suggests a Kievan influence, often found in churches of the Ternopil' cruciform style. It was renovated in the mid-1980s. Before renovation, there were smaller domes on the gables, which may be a reflection of the Hutsul style.

The church was built in 1919 by Anton Prychun, at a cost of $6,000. It replaced an earlier building erected in 1909, which was subsequently used as a parish hall. There is a bell tower on the property, on which one of the original small domes has been placed, and the cemetery is about two kilometres to the south.

St. John the Baptist Ukrainian Catholic Church, Dolyny

Although St. John the Baptist Church [fig. 4.31] is essentially built in a Ternopil' cruciform style with a large open dome at the centre of a cruciform structure, the Kievan influence is apparent in the shape of the onion domes. The location of the smaller domes at the gables suggests a Hutsul influence not uncommon in churches of this style.

4.31 St. John the Baptist Church, Dolyny

Construction of the church was begun in 1904 by builders John and Peter Koltutsky. It was consecrated in 1907. The carved iconostasis dates from 1928. The walls feature icons by Jacob Maydanyk; the icons are framed with Ukrainian embroidery motifs. The stained glass for a number of the windows was donated by individual parishioners. The whole interior is adorned with *faux marble* (wood and plaster painted to resemble marble), and various decorative motifs.

St. Michael's Ukrainian Orthodox Church, Sandy Lake

St. Michael's Church in Sandy Lake is another fine example of a church built in the Ternopil' cruciform style [fig.4.32]. It has a massive central dome. The overall decorative treatment is of Cossack baroque inspiration. The two towers at the front are a non-traditional baroque facade treatment common in Manitoba (see chapter 5). There is an elaborate bell tower on the property.

72

4.32 St. Michael's Church, Sandy Lake

St. Michael's Parish was organized in 1927, and held services in a rented Anglican Church for several years. The parish acquired the building in 1933 and converted it to a Ukrainian Orthodox church. The iconostasis was painted by Hnat Sych in 1941. It was destroyed by fire in 1944, and a new building was begun immediately under the supervision of Alex Semanyk, chief carpenter. It was consecrated in 1948. The iconostasis, built by Kipra, was painted by Olga Moroz. The iconography and decoration of the interior of the church are by Dmytro Bartoshuk.

MANITOBA VARIATIONS

5

THE BUILDERS OF UKRAINIAN CHURCHES in Manitoba responded to the conditions they encountered in the new land by creating certain architectural variations to traditional styles. But at the same time they retained strong cultural and personal links with their past, and the churches have retained their essentially Byzantine spirit.

As the newly arrived immigrants adapted to Canadian conditions, local cultural factors began influencing the building of churches. Sometimes these factors were easily accommodated; for example, the immigrants had to find new ways to use new building materials. Very often, however, the factors were complex. For example, the immigrants found new architectural styles in the new land – styles with elements foreign to Ukrainian tradition – and sometimes the architectural form of the new church was affected by the borrowing of these new styles. For instance, Russian church architecture – a legacy of the Russian Ortho-dox Mission, which operated in Manitoba during the first thirty years of this century – strongly influenced the style of some Ukrainian churches in Manitoba.

With the passage of time, perhaps over two or three generations, the need for Ukrainian churches to conform strictly to traditional architectural models seemed less compelling: to the younger genera-tion, place memories of the old country were becoming vague, and so was the attachment to traditional forms. Also, as the general level of education improved, people found architectural inspiration in published materials. Hence, many churches were built that, although unmistakably of Byzantine lineage, defy classification. For our purposes here, they are called Manitoba variations.

THE TWO-TOWER PATTERN

A striking and quite common deviation from traditional styles is the addition of twin towers on the facades of Ukrainian churches in Manitoba. At first glance, these towers appear as a western European Gothic influence that was widespread among Roman Catholic churches in Poland and Slovakia. However, a survey of church architecture in Ukraine has yielded only isolated examples of the two-tower configuration, and these are limited to a few Ukrainian Catholic churches in western Ukraine where the Polish influence was strong, or to a few churches in the Kiev-Poltava region designed by "westernizing" architects.

The two-tower pattern developed in Manitoba into a decorative device in its own right, and has become an accepted architectural form in Canadian Ukrainian churches. There are two explanations for this. First, the addition to the facade of two small corner columns, each surmounted by an onion dome, was an inexpensive means to lend instant identity to a simple frame building. Second, Fr. Philip Ruh, whose architectural work has profoundly influenced Ukrainian church architecture on the prairies, favoured the design.

5.1 **Church of the Ascension of Our Lord, Ukraina**

Ascension of Our Lord Ukrainian Catholic Church, Ukraina

The Church of the Ascension of Our Lord in Ukraina [fig. 5.1] illustrates the most simple way that the addition of two corner pilasters surmounted by onion domes immediately lends an identity to a structure and characterizes it as an eastern European church. This was achieved at little cost and did not affect the structure in any way.

The parish was founded in 1916 and a church was built the following year. In June 1927, the church was knocked over by a storm and immediately re-erected using materials salvaged from the collapsed church. The man in charge of construction was Dmytro Rymiak. There is a bell tower on the church grounds (built in the 1930s), as well as a cemetery. Due to the migration of parishioners to the town of Dauphin, the parish has dissolved and the church is officially closed.

5.2 Church of the Ascension of Our Lord, Petlura

Ascension of Our Lord Ukrainian Catholic Church, Petlura

The Church of the Ascension of Our Lord in Petlura [fig. 5.2] has two corner towers in the facade. Instead of using onion domes, the builders covered the towers with flowing-form roofs reminiscent of the traditional shapes. As in the the church in Ukraina, the two towers affect the structural aspects of the building very little. The three-chambered plan suggests a traditional Boyko model.

The parish was founded in 1929, when land was acquired for the construction of the church. It was completed in 1936. Andrew Matskiw and Theodore Novosad were the builders. There is a bell tower nearby.

THE THREE-TOWER PATTERN

The three-tower pattern is often encountered in Ukrainian churches in Manitoba; it is significant because of the theological symbolism associated with the number three. It represents the Trinity, or it may represent the deisis: Christ on the Cross with the Theotokos and St. John by His side.

Historically, there had been two essentially distinct ways to view church architecture. Byzantine architects conceived a building as a mass, as a geometric volume in space; hence there was a strong emphasis on the overall shape and balance of the building, and on its roofline. In contrast, baroque architects emphasized the importance of the facade, where most of the decorative elements were concentrated. In Manitoba, both of these approaches exist. Churches with their principal tower located over the body of the building reflect the Byzantine concept; they often conceal an interior dome, but the structural systems required to support the additional load require more elaborate construction methods. Churches with all three towers located along the facade reflect a baroque influence. This configuration presents obvious structural advantages: an elaborate facade can be added to a relatively simple building, or incorporated into the design without requiring any special means to handle structural stresses.

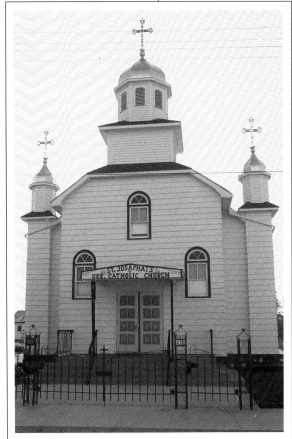

5.3 St. Josaphat Church, Shoal Lake

St. Josaphat Ukrainian Catholic Church, Shoal Lake

St. Josaphat Church [fig. 5.3] has three towers along the facade. The facade is rather elaborate, but the main body of the church is simple and unencumbered. The structural problems that would arise from putting a heavy load on a wide span have been resolved by placing the main tower, which is rather large for this configuration, over a much narrower element of the building. St. Josaphat Church was built in 1945 by Steve Borody. The iconography is by Jacob Maydanyk.

5.4 Holy Ghost Church, Winnipeg

Holy Ghost Ukrainian Catholic Church, Winnipeg

Holy Ghost Church in Winnipeg [fig. 5.4] is another simple-gable building that has been given its identity by a three-tower facade. The main tower is located over the front wall, adding little stress to the roof, and the two side domes are located over corner pilasters. The domes are executed in Cossack baroque style.

The church was built in 1932, at a cost of $4,000, to serve the local Ukrainian population of Brooklands, most of whom were employed in the nearby CPR yards. P. Marykuca was head designer and carpenter, and he was assisted by S. Burdy and K. Bendzelak. The paintings and iconography were done by Jacob Maydanyk in the 1940s. There is a bell tower, housing two bells, on the grounds. The church was extensively renovated in 1980. The parish serves about fifty families, the majority of whom can trace their origins to Galicia.

Ukrainian Catholic Church of the Holy Ghost, Merridale

The builders of the Church of the Holy Ghost [fig. 5.5] emphasized the three-dimensional aspect of the building rather than the facade. The central tower was constructed rather lightly, in order not to stress the gable roof. The two side domes were placed on pilasters, and an apse and a small narthex were added to the basic nave. The three-chamber layout suggests a Boyko influence.

The church was built in 1923 at a cost of $3,500. There are a well-designed bell tower and a cemetery on the church grounds.

5.5 Church of the Holy Ghost, Merridale

Ukrainian Orthodox Church of the Transfiguration, Menzie

The two towers are not an integral part of the facade on the Church of the Transfiguration [fig. 5.6]; rather, they are part of the nave. The decorative treatment over the entrance diminishes the angular effect of the gable roof, and the three-dimensional aspect of the church is emphasized. The main dome positioned on the centre of the gable roof required some reinforcing of the rafters to support the load and prevent the spreading of the walls – a common problem in this configuration.

Although Ukrainians began settling in the Menzie area in 1898, the Church of the Transfiguration was not built until 1925, after the organization of the Ukrainian Orthodox Church of Canada. There is a very attractive bell tower on the grounds.

Ukrainian Orthodox Church of the Ascension, Angusville

Byzantine and baroque influences meet in the Church of the Ascension [fig. 5.7]: the respective location of the domes is three-dimensional; at

5.6 Church of the Transfiguration, Menzie

5.7 Church of the Ascension, Angusville

5.8   Church of the Holy Eucharist, Rosa

the same time the facade is given some prominence. The placement of the central dome over the nave causes some construction difficulties because of the additional weight it creates. The arched false front and vaulted canopy over the entrance give the building a certain Kievan-Byzantine flavour.

CRUCIFORM CHURCHES

A number of churches in Manitoba, while having retained the basic Byzantine cruciform floor plan found in traditional Kievan, Hutsul and Ternopil' churches, contain other features that distinguish them from the "old-country" models. The basic cruciform appearance of a church might have been changed, for example, by the addition of two towers or an elaborate facade.

Holy Eucharist Ukrainian Catholic Church, Rosa
The main body of the Church of the Holy Eucharist [fig. 5.8] was laid out according to a cruciform plan and is surmounted by a small dome, which suggests a Hutsul configuration common around Stuartburn. However, the longer nave, the two towers at the front, and the vestibule, or narthex, alter the style of the building from the traditional.

The Holy Eucharist Parish was founded in 1924 and construction was begun the same year. Skrynskyi and Zvizdark were the builders. The interior was completed in 1933. Hnat Sych and B. Kohut did the artwork. A well-kept cemetery and bell tower are on the property. New aluminum siding, installed in 1982, replaces the original imitation brick siding.

St. George's Ukrainian Orthodox Church, Dauphin
Built of masonry, St. George's Church [fig. 5.9] has an elongated cruciform floor plan that is traditional in form. The large dome at the centre suggests a Ternopil' influence, and the domes are treated in a Kievan baroque manner. There are, however, two large towers at the

5.9 St. George's Church, Dauphin, exterior view.

5.10 St. George's Church, Dauphin; detail of the artwork on the iconostasis.

5.11 St. Volodymyr Church, Oakburn

front of the church and an elaborate facade, both of which, although Byzantine in spirit, deviate from the traditional form. This church is a good illustration of how the two-tower/facade pattern evolved from wood to large masonry construction. The finely carved iconostasis is of particular interest [fig. 5.10].

St. George's Church was built between 1959 and 1962 and is the second church in the history of the parish. The building was designed by Vasyl Grodzyk and built by Freiheit Construction Company. The interior was designed by Dmytro Bartoshuk of Winnipeg, and the iconostasis by Kostas Papadakis of Minneapolis. The bell tower was donated in 1969 by Mr. and Mrs. M. Demchuk. The church cemetery is located two miles south of Dauphin.

St. Volodymyr Ukrainian Orthodox Church, Oakburn

The appearance of St. Volodymyr Church [fig. 5.11] suggests that collective image and place memory figured prominently in its design. The cruciform layout of the main body of the church, surmounted by a large central dome, is of the Ternopil' cruciform style, but the rounded apse is not typical. The multitude of domes gives the church a definite Kievan flavour, but the three-tower facade is more baroque in nature. The enclosed entrance makes good sense in our climate, but it is not of a traditional Ukrainian style.

The church was built in 1947. The bell tower is located near the church.

St. Michael's Ukrainian Catholic Church, Olha

St. Michael's Church [fig. 5.12] is characterized by two large towers on its facade (the roof of which suggests a dome in rather a unique way), a small decorative dome at its centre that is not open to the interior, and conchae on its sides. It is a blend of Hutsul, baroque and some western European ecclesiastical architectural styles.

Erected in 1904 under the supervision of John and Peter Koltutsky at a cost of approximately $2,000, this impressive church reflects the ambitious hopes of a pioneer community less than a decade old. Much of the labour was volunteer and, as the small cost indicates, most of the material was likely donated.

5.12 St. Michael's Church, Olha

The interior of St. Michael's Church features many icons painted by Jacob Maydanyk. The iconostasis is intricately carved and decorated with Ukrainian emboidery motifs.

ECLECTIC STYLES

There are a number of Ukrainian churches in Manitoba that do not conform to any particular classification; rather, they embody a combination of architectural styles. The design of these churches reflects a particular blend of the place memories of the immigrants who imagined them, the creativity and ingenuity of the people who built them, and the local styles of Manitoba churches of other denominations.

St. Anthony Petchersky Ukrainian Catholic Church, Lac du Bonnet

St. Anthony Petchersky Church [fig. 5.13] illustrates one of the many imaginative ways that a simple gable-roof structure might be given a Byzantine flavour. It was designed by Fr. Hewko and built by volunteer labour in 1937. Originally located in Brightstone, it was moved to Lac du Bonnet in 1960 and rededicated in 1961.

Holy Ghost Ukrainian Orthodox Church, Petlura

The Church of the Holy Ghost in Petlura [fig. 5.14] does not relate to any specific traditional style. It is believed that the designer, Michael Swystun, patterned the church after a photograph of a church in Kiev; hence, there is a strong suggestion of the superstructure of St. Sophia's Cathedral [see fig. 2.18]. The large dome surrounded by four smaller corner domes is a Kievan pattern, symbolizing Christ and the four evangelists. The way the designer has integrated the two front towers into the facade is noteworthy, as are the semi-circular arches, which lend the church a Byzantine flavour. The porch is a later, utilitarian addition.

The church replaces an earlier, simpler structure that stood next to the present one. Construction began in 1943 and was completed in 1961. Lack of funds was the major reason for the lengthy construction period. Swystun was paid sixty cents per hour for his work. It was the last church he built. It is situated on a four-acre lot donated by Tom Bezza. Walter Symchych designed and constructed the iconostasis.

5.13 St. Anthony Petchersky Church, Lac du Bonnet

5.14 Church of the Holy Ghost, Petlura

5.15 Sts. Peter and Paul Church, Seech

Sts. Peter and Paul Ukrainian Orthodox Church, Seech

The large domes adorning Sts. Peter and Paul Church [fig. 5.15] give it a Kievan flavour, which is reinforced by the arched motif in the facade. The Gothic influence in the two front towers is quite pronounced. The building does not relate to any pure Ukrainian church tradition. The arch motif in the facade is purely ornamental and appears in other churches designed by the same builder.

Sts. Peter and Paul Church was built in 1937. It was designed by Michael Swystun and built by him with the help of ten volunteers. Olga Moroz did the interior artwork. There is a large bell tower near the church.

Immaculate Conception Ukrainian Catholic Church, Cooks Creek

The Church of the Immaculate Conception [fig. 5.16] was begun in 1930 by Fr. Philip Ruh. In designing his churches, he endeavoured to reflect the Ukrainian tradition as he experienced it in Galicia, where he developed an affinity for Byzantine and traditional Ukrainian church architecture. However, he needed to satisfy the liturgical needs of a Ukrainian Catholic parish, which at that time was subjected to latinizing influences. Moreover, because Ruh spent his formative years in his native Lorraine, a strong Gothic architectural tradition was imprinted upon him. The result was a unique and very personal eclecticism, which the Church of the Immaculate Conception illustrates better than any other of Fr. Ruh's designs. The overall silhouette, with its multitude of domes, is of early Kievan inspiration. The windows and decorative designs on the exterior walls are Romanesque, while the portico and the spacious nave are strongly reminiscent of the Gothic cathedrals.

Cook's Creek Parish was founded in 1929. Construction of the church commenced in 1930 and was completed in 1952. The Church of the Immaculate Conception was the parish's first church and remains in use today, although it is used only two or three times per year. Fr. Ruh

5.16 **Church of the Immaculate Conception, Cooks Creek**

5.17 Church of the Holy Trinity, Gonor

involved himself in the actual work of construction, along with the parishioners who also volunteered their labour. Fr. Ruh wrote on one of the blueprints (framed and displayed in the interior of the church), describing some of the problems he encountered during the building phases: "In 1932-38 the years were poor. There were a lot of grasshoppers and it was very dry. Because of the lack of prosperity the church was built slowly following a cash base." Fr. Ruh's constant encouragement gave the people hope, which in turn fed their determination. A grotto, which is a replica of the grotto in Lourdes, France, and which is named Our Lady of Lourdes, has been built next to the church. It contains a Calvary and the Stations of the Cross. It was completed in 1954, and a pilgrimage to the grotto is held every August in honour of the Blessed Virgin Mary.

The Church of the Immaculate Conception has been designated as an historic site.[1]

Holy Trinity Ukrainian Catholic Church, Gonor

The Church of the Holy Trinity [fig. 5.17], built according to a cruciform floor plan with two towers at the front, is one of the churches designed by Fr. Ruh that exhibits the greatest Gothic influence (or perhaps the greatest international influence, as some researchers have noted). Fr. Ruh died before the completion of this church. The design work was completed by architect Victor Deneka, who endeavoured to impart a Kievan-Byzantine flavour by capping the towers with domes. This church is remarkable because it is the first church in which stainless steel was used for the domes.

5.18 Church of the Ascension, Winnipegosis

The parish was founded in 1899, when the original church was built. The original church was one of the best examples in Manitoba of a church built in the the Hutsul style. The old church was razed in 1952 to make room for construction of the present building.

Ukrainian Catholic Church of the Ascension, Winnipegosis
The Church of the Ascension [fig. 5.18], built in 1929, is another fine example of Fr. Ruh's eclectic design. It illustrates his capacity for invention within the confines of his standardized church design. Like nearly all of his churches, the building is cruciform; it has three domes, two as facade towers, and one at the central crossing; it is baroque in outline and in decorative power. Originally covered with alternating bands of shingles of different colours, the structure was a visual feast.

The tall central dome was struck by lightning in the late 1970s and was rebuilt soon afterwards; unfortunately, however, it was made lower, thus destroying the original proportions. At the same time, the domes and the roof were reshingled, and the colourful bands gave way to a more sombre rendering. Still, the building is a notable example of Fr. Ruh's work.

ACQUIRED CHURCH BUILDINGS

Although Ukrainian congregations ideally wanted to build their own churches in traditional styles, it was often impractical or financially impossible. Occasionally, church buildings designed for other denominations would become available for sale at reasonable prices. In each case, the existing buildings had to be adapted to accommodate the liturgical needs and tradition of the new owners. There are several such churches in Manitoba.

Ukrainian Greek Orthodox Cathedral of St. John Suchavsky, Winnipeg

St. John Suchavsky Cathedral [fig. 5.19] operates under the jurisdiction of the Bishop of the Ukrainian Orthodox Church in America and Canada, which in turn operates under the Ecumenical Patriarchate of Constantinople.

5.19 St. John Suchavsky Cathedral, Winnipeg

The structure was built by the congregation of McGregor United Methodists between 1850 and 1884. The Brotherhood of St. Ivan (John) Suchavsky purchased the building in 1931 for $5,000, raising the money through voluntary contributions ($1,000) and loans (another $1,000) among the members, and obtaining a mortgage of $3,000. It was built in Norman-Gothic architectural style, typical of Canadian Protestant churches of the period. The new congregation rebuilt the roof with the addition of Kievan-style domes, and added a sanctuary. The interior of the cathedral contains an iconostasis that was originally built by George Billas. The first icons were painted by Hnat Sych. In 1966 the iconostasis was repainted and the icons were replaced, the new icons done in the style of western realism by Mrs. E. Stachursky. The altar was built by Vasyl Hordy. In 1933, through the efforts of Rev. Fr. John Zazulak and Vasyl Hordy, bells for the belfry were donated by the CPR. Later, electronic bells were donated by Mr. and Mrs. Safriuk. The old bells are used only on special holidays.

St. Michael Ukrainian Orthodox Church, Winnipeg

St. Michael Church [fig. 5.20], was adapted for Orthodox use from an Anglican church. The conversion to Orthodox use consisted of the addition of a bell tower and the building of an onion dome over the porch; this gave it a somewhat Lemko-like appearance. The construction of an iconostasis and a raised sanctuary area completed the interior conversion. The basement, which is larger than the building itself, contains a large parish hall that includes a well-appointed stage.

The parish was founded in 1918 and was originally served by Russian Orthodox missionaries. A great majority of the early parishioners were employees of the CPR, who applied their skills and used scrap materials to build the liturgical necessities of the church. For example, the royal doors were fashioned out of heavy-gauge sheet metal. The parish joined the Ukrainian Greek Orthodox Church of Canada in 1932. At that time, there was a large Ukrainian population in the area, and the parish thrived. With the aging and migration of the original parishioners, the congregation has dwindled to about fifteen families, a fact not reflected at the weekly services, since non-parishioners often attend.

5.20 St. Michael Church, Winnipeg

CONTEMPORARY MANITOBA CHURCHES

6

THERE ARE IN MANITOBA and throughout the prairies an increasing number of churches conceived by contemporary designers who, in various ways, have endeavoured to translate traditional architecture into modern forms either through the use of modern idioms, or by adapting modern techniques. The search has taken many paths. Some designers have used traditional models, some have opted for new and experimental architectural forms, some have selectively incorporated forms and motifs into the structure of a contemporary building, while others have chosen merely to append traditional-looking features to thoroughly functional contemporary buildings.

Holy Ghost Ukrainian Catholic Church, Beausejour
Holy Ghost Church in Beausejour [fig. 6.1] is an example of a church in which a conscious effort has been made by a contemporary architect to return to the roots of traditional early Christian architectural forms. It is a domed basilica of Byzantine style, made with modern materials. What lends this church a particularly Byzantine flavour is the central dome, which appears suspended above the windows of the drum, and the treatment of the arched facade. Designed by Manitoba architect Victor Deneka, it was built in 1964 primarily by volunteer parishioners. The iconostasis, designed and painted by artist Igor Suhacev, was added

later. Roman Kowal did the stained-glass work and artist Colsan painted the stations of the cross.

The church was built to replace the old one, which was built in 1905 and had been damaged several times by high winds. It was also poorly located, being separated from the community by railway tracks and hidden behind grain elevators. The parishioners of Holy Ghost Church worked extremely hard to raise the $75,000 needed to build it: the women ran a catering service and raised $50,000; the men ran bingos and raised $25,000. The land on which the church was to be built was swampy and needed fill; the parishioners provided it. They also provided their labour for construction, a unique event for the 1960s. The date of completion – August 23, 1964 – is inscribed on the cornerstone. In addition to the church structure itself, a residence for the priest was constructed.

6.1 Holy Ghost Church, Beausejour

St. Nicholas Ukrainian Catholic Church, Winnipeg

St. Nicholas Church [fig. 6.2] is a contemporary interpretation of the Byzantine style, done with modern materials and building techniques. It was designed by architects Alex Nitchuk and Bernard Brown. The central dome is appropriately symbolic. However, the four large corner globes, although aesthetically pleasing, fail to convey any traditional meaning or function other than a hint of Kievan style. The structure is reminiscent of the top portion of the Synagogue of Florence, which is considered a textbook example of late Byzantine architecture, and which points to the probability of considerable research on the part of the designers. It is on the whole a rather impressive building.

St. Nicholas Parish is the oldest Ukrainian Catholic parish in Winnipeg; it was organized in 1899. The present church structure on the corner of Arlington and Bannerman is the third structure in the history of the parish. In 1961 the parish purchased eleven lots containing war-time houses for $116,900; in 1964 the old houses were torn down and construction of the church began. The parish built a monastery on the site at the same time. This monastery became the provincial headquarters for the Basilian Fathers who, in 1958, had moved from Edmonton to Winnipeg. Both church and monastery were completed in the summer of 1966. The total cost was approximately $650,000.

6.2 St. Nicholas Church, Winnipeg

Holy Trinity Ukrainian Orthodox Cathedral, Winnipeg

Holy Trinity Cathedral [fig. 6.3] is a building of relatively simple design made to look traditional by the addition of falsework on the structural roof. The cathedral is a well-known Winnipeg landmark, with its five onion domes in a well-rendered Kievan baroque style. However, these domes are not an integral part of the building and cannot be detected from the interior. Traditionally, the dome should be visible from the inside, performing a liturgical and symbolic function (see chapter 2). The interior of the cathedral is well-appointed, but in search of modernism, the designer lent the iconostasis an art deco flavour, and the second-storey galleries are foreign to the Orthodox tradition.

The cathedral is the seat of the metropolitan bishop, who is the spiritual head of the Ukrainian Orthodox Church of Canada. The parish was organized in 1946 and a site was purchased the same year. A worldwide design competition was held and forty sketches were submitted.

The entry by George Korbyn and Alexander Powstenko, entitled "Kiev," was chosen and adopted as the basis for the design of the cathedral. Using the "Kiev" sketch as a model, architects Pratt and Ross of Winnipeg designed the basement of the cathedral; contruction was begun in 1949 and completed in 1952. The cathedral proper was designed by Winnipeg architect Alex W. Nitchuk, who based his design on the "Kiev" sketch as well. Construction of the upper level (the cathedral) was begun in 1957 and completed in 1962. The total cost was $600,000. The first pontifical liturgy was officiated by Metropolitan Ilarion on January 7, 1962.

6.3 Holy Trinity Cathedral, Winnipeg

St. Joseph's Ukrainian Catholic Church, Winnipeg

St. Joseph's Church is another simple structural shell that is adorned with non-functional towers placed on a flat concrete roof to lend the building an identity [fig. 6.4]. It was designed by architect Radoslav Zuk.

St. Joseph's Parish was the eleventh Ukrainian Catholic parish to be established in greater Winnipeg and the first in Canada to be named in honour of St. Joseph. St. Joseph's German Catholic Men's Club offered the parish the use of their hall until a church could be built, and the Ukrainians used it for their liturgies and social functions from 1952 to 1954. In early 1954, the parish purchased some property at the corner of Aikins and Jefferson for $5,000. The sod-turning ceremony was held July 11, 1954. Alex W. Nitchuk designed the basement. Rev. Fr. Joseph Denischuk headed a three-month campaign to collect funds. The parishioners donated about $4,000, and they borrowed about $15,000. The basement was completed in the fall of 1954 and was used for all church activities, including spiritual functions, until 1958. During that

6.4 St. Joseph's Church, Winnipeg

year the basement was extended on both the north and south sides, and plans for the church proper were drawn up. In the spring of 1962 a loan of $200,000 was obtained for the construction of the upper portion. Semmler Construction Company was hired to build the church and it was completed in late 1963; the opening celebration was held in December of that year.

Sts. Vladimir and Olga Ukrainian Catholic Cathedral, Winnipeg

Sts. Vladimir and Olga Cathedral [fig. 6.5] is essentially a conventional Roman basilica design. It is rather simple in its form, and the Byzantine flavour has been achieved (though only partially) by the addition of hemispherical domes surmounting two non-functional towers at the front. A sense of the traditional is lent, primarily internally, by the elaborate Eastern-rite iconostasis and exuberant artwork.

Although the present structure is the third building to house the congregation, there is an historical continuity, for much of the artwork from the previous buildings has been incorporated into the present Sts. Vladimir and Olga Cathedral. The fact that each building was built larger than its predecessor attests to the growth and stability of a congregation that, through the years, has been the major cultural stronghold of the Ukrainian community in Winnipeg. The second building, located on the same site, is now used as a parish hall.

The present structure was designed by Col. J.N. Semmens and was constructed between 1948 and 1951. As the episcopal seat of the Ukrainian Catholic Church for Winnipeg, Sts. Vladimir and Olga Cathedral has been richly adorned with interior artwork, lending it appropriate prestige. The interior artwork was done by Sviatoslav Hordynsky, an

101

6.6 Holy Family Church, Winnipeg

6.5 Sts. Vladimir and Olga Cathedral, Winnipeg

iconographer based in New York, by R. Pachowsky and I. Wolaniuk, also from the United States, and by Roman Kowal, a Winnipeg artist. The iconostasis is the work of Serhij Lytwynenko, who is also responsible for two bronze plaques in the vestibule, commemorating the opening of the cathedral and honouring the long and diligent service of one of the parish priests, Fr. Wasyl Kushnir. The windows on the sides of the church are particularly important because of their size, their subject matter, and the calibre of the artists who did them (see figs. 7.30 and A.18).

Holy Family Ukrainian Catholic Church, Winnipeg

The Holy Family Church is characterized by a trapezoidal floor plan; the elevated portion over the altar area is in the form of three glazed arches; and there is a series of smaller pre-cast arches at the entrance [fig. 6.6]. It was designed by architect Radoslav Zuk. The glazed arches were particularly impressive when catching the late afternoon sun; unfortunately, a new high-rise building now stands in the way, and the effect is no longer achievable. However, the arches do convey a certain traditional flavour, another effect the architect was endeavouring to achieve.

The Holy Family Parish was organized during the early 1930s. Between 1932 and 1935 Kobzar Hall, a Ukrainian cultural club, was used for liturgies and other church functions. The first church was built in 1935 on the corner of Lilac and Scotland. It served as a mission church between 1935 and 1947. The new church was built and completed during 1962 and 1963, just three blocks west of the old one. It was constructed by a combination of hired and volunteer labour.

6.7 St. Michael and the Angels Church, Tyndall

St. Michael and the Angels Ukrainian Catholic Church, Tyndall

St. Michael and the Angels Church in Tyndall[1] [fig. 6.7] is very similar in design to the Holy Family Church in Winnipeg. Although the church is quite modern in its overall concept, architect Radoslav Zuk was particularly successful in capturing the spirit of a traditional church of the Boyko region. There is an elevated portion over the sanctuary, topped by three peaks. The dominance of the central peak and the materials used, combined with the setting, along a row of tall spruce trees, create a distinct sense of place.

The Tyndall church was built in 1962, to replace an older, wooden structure erected in 1917. The parish priest, Fr. M. Kotowich, worked as the head carpenter and did much of the carpentry himself. Original costs for the building in 1960 were $14,000. Parish activity declined during the 1970s, and liturgies are now held only once or twice a month.

6.8 All Saints Church, Winnipeg

All Saints Ukrainian Orthodox Church, Winnipeg

All Saints Church [fig. 6.8] is an example of the way in which decorative treatment of the facade lends identity to a standard industrial shell, a glue-laminated arch building in this case.

The parish was organized in the early 1920s when many Ukrainians were settling in the Transcona area. At first, the liturgies were celebrated about once a month and were often held in the Taras Shevchenko National Home in Transcona, which the congration was able to purchase in 1957 for $2,000. The parish wanted to build its own church, however, so plans were made to purchase some land. In early 1964 they bought and blessed a plot of land on Day Street, and later that year they built the church.

MAJOR MANITOBA
UKRAINIAN ARTISTS

7

THE MEN AND WOMEN who actually produced the Ukrainian churches of Manitoba were led in this work by a small but significant group of skilled people.[1] Some of them were professionally trained, but most were not. For the most part, their individual stories are buried in the memories of those who knew and worked with them. Seldom did they leave any documentation of their lives and work. As a group, they formed something like an extended family whose connections reach far and wide throughout Manitoba's and Canada's architectural and artistic history. It is clear in the research to date that many of these skilled workers knew and admired each other's work; younger ones were apprenticed to older ones in their field, and the vast majority of them taught themselves and passed their skills on to willing followers. Their sources of inspiration to do the design, construction and decoration of Ukrainian churches seemed to be their awareness of the great need for this work, their love of their craft, and, for many, a deep faith and devotion to the church of their choice. This is all the more important when we consider that most of them had only memories of homeland churches, some holy books and pictures, and the wishes of the congregation for whom they worked to guide them in their work.

ARCHITECTS

In the period before the Second World War, the Ukrainians in Manitoba did not hire professional architects to design their churches. Only a few men who gained a reputation for their designing and drafting skills and who had some semi-professional training fulfilled the role of architect. In this pioneering period, the designer was often construction manager as well. He was responsible to a building committee of the parish and had to come to agreement on size, style and building materials to be used for the church, and be generally sensitive to the needs of the congregation. As well, he was required to keep accounts and report to the parish on progress.

In the period following the Second World War, Ukrainian congregations began hiring trained architects to design their churches. They also began to conform to the prevailing practice of tendering contracts.

Fr. Philip Ruh

Philip Ruh [fig. 7.1] is perhaps the most interesting and colourful of all the individuals involved in the design and construction of Ukrainian churches in Manitoba in the twentieth century.[2] His roots were non-Ukrainian but his fervent religious feelings and deep attachment to the Ukrainian people and their traditions served to produce some of the most impressive church architecture in this province.

Born in 1883 in a village in Lorraine, France, the second of ten children of a farmer,

7.1 Rev. Fr. Philip Ruh, O.M.I. (courtesy P. Ruh Collection UCEC)

7.2 Destroyed by fire in 1966, St. Mary's Church in Mountain Road was the first of Fr. Ruh's structures described as the "prairie cathedral" (courtesy St. Mary's Church).

Philip Ruh accomplished his dreams of becoming a missionary priest when he was ordained into the Oblate Order in 1910. He was then sent to Galicia for two years to become acquainted with the language and lifestyle of Ukrainians there before being transferred in 1913 to work among the Ukrainians on the Canadian prairies. He served the scattered Ukrainian population from his base in northern Alberta for ten years, on a thousand-mile circuit, enduring all the hardships of a pioneer. His seminary education included some rudimentary training in architectural principles, so when he was called upon by the Basilian Fathers with whom he worked to design and build chapels, churches and other necessary buildings, he was willing and able to help. By 1923 he had gained a reputation for his skill as an architect, and was being sought in other parts of Canada and the United States.

The first church he built in Manitoba was St. Mary's Church in Mountain Road [fig. 7.2]; it was begun in 1923. He was young, enthusiastic and something of a visionary. Relying on his memory of some of the large churches he had become familiar with in Galicia, he designed and completed the first of his "prairie cathedrals," all within one year. The exact origin of the term *prairie cathedral* is not clear. However, it has come to be applied to Ruh's large churches in Mountain Road, Portage la Prairie [fig. 7.3], Dauphin and Cooks Creek[3] (as well as one in Edmonton) because of their remarkable size and grandeur. Ruh designed many more Manitoba churches, but of smaller dimensions than these four.

The inspiration for Ruh's work came from his love of his adopted people, whose language and customs he learned and used faithfully. Always a good learner, he probably recalled easily his impressions of

Galician and other churches he'd seen, and combined these impressions with the requirements of the congregations he worked for. Ruh was known to have been a good manager of resources and people, a likeable, energetic man who could motivate others, by example, to long hours of hard work [fig. 7.4]. He never claimed to have had any formal architectural or engineering education, but this did not deter him from producing many beautiful church structures on this continent. After Ruh became parish priest of Cooks Creek in 1930 he was more an architect and less a builder than he had been in the 1920s. His favourite master builders, Mike Yanchynski [fig. 7.5] and Mike Sawchuk, grew to understand his plans and drawings so well that they could later build churches from them with little guidance from Ruh himself.

7.3 **The Church of the Assumption of the Blessed Virgin Mary in Portage la Prairie was one of Fr. Ruh's early churches. It was razed in 1983 to make room for the parking lot of the newly built church, seen in the left background.**

The style of churches Ruh built was clearly drawn from the Ukrainian Catholic churches of Galicia. He incorporated Ukrainian architectural traditions with the size and grandeur of some western European cathedrals he knew. He created the space for the fullest expression of the painters' and artists' talents who adorned the churches he built.

Ruh was also known as a healer, a dedicated priest and a good friend to many. He died in 1962 in Winnipeg and is buried in the graveyard near his parish church in Cooks Creek, Manitoba.

Victor Deneka
Victor Deneka [fig. 7.6] is one of the most prominent post–Second World War church architects in Manitoba. He was born in Samarkand of Ukrainian parents and came to Canada in 1949. He studied at the Carolo-

7.4 Volunteers building a church on the prairie, with Fr. Ruh standing behind, directing and building with the parishioners (courtesy P. Ruh Collection UCEC).

7.5 Mary and Michael Yanchynski with Fr. Ruh in the Yanchynski home, Cooks Creek, ca. 1935 (courtesy P. Ruh Collection UCEC).

7.6 Victor Deneka, architect (courtesy V. Deneka)

Wilhelmina Technical University, Braunschweig, Germany, and the University of Manitoba, where he obtained a Bachelor of Architecture degree in 1952. Besides following a career at the CNR as regional architect of the prairie region, he had a private practice and was often commissioned to design churches. He designed eight Ukrainian Catholic churches in Manitoba and re-designed several others, and he also designed church fronts, bell towers and domes. According to his own assessment of his work, Deneka attempted to blend traditional elements with the potential he perceived in new materials, and to mold them as an expression of local worship and liturgical practices. He has given a number of lectures on the topic of Ukrainian church architecture, notably to the 1987 gathering of the Canadian Learned Societies in Hamilton, Ontario.

Radoslav Zuk

Radoslav Zuk [fig. 7.7] is a Canadian architect with a professional background and Ukrainian roots. He was born and raised in Lubachiv in western Ukraine. He received his Bachelor of Architecture degree from McGill University (with honours) in 1957, and his Master's at the Massachusetts Institute of Technology in 1960. Upon graduation in 1960 he began his academic career teaching at the University of Manitoba, and then went on to McGill where he still teaches. Simultaneously with his teaching career he has designed nine Ukrainian churches, four of which are in Manitoba.

Zuk's work in general is in keeping with certain objectives he has defined. He believes that the church ought to reflect Ukrainian traditional architecture, to provide for the main liturgical functions, and to be responsive to its contemporary surroundings. When the parishes he worked for decided to erect the church themselves rather than hire a contracting company, his additional objective was to design a simple structure using easily-obtained building materials. Zuk believed that church architecture should maintain the traditional images and meanings of Ukrainian culture, and at the same time be appropriate for the

7.7 Radoslav Zuk, architect
(courtesy R. Zuk)

7.8 Michael Sawchuk, builder, 1950
(courtesy Mrs. K. Kuzyk, Winnipeg)

geography and contemporary environment in which it is located. In his own words, "The task then is to create an architecture which responds to a specific cultural temperament and historical experience, yet is expressive of the given geographic situation and of the dynamics of the contemporary spirit."[4]

Zuk's churches are certainly distinctive landmarks in the towns and cities where they are located. To the lay person these churches may appear ultramodern or strange; certain elements may appear to be radical departures from the norms of Ukrainian church architecture. On closer examination, however, one sees that his designs do indeed incorporate Ukrainian traditions, although in a unique, stylized manner.

MASTER BUILDERS

Michael Sawchuk
Michael Sawchuk [fig. 7.8] was a close friend and associate of Fr. Philip Ruh and master builder Michael Yanchynski, and was involved with them in the construction of several Ukrainian churches in Manitoba.

Sawchuk was born in 1900 in Mountain Road, Manitoba, the fourth of five children. His parents had emigrated from Chortkiv county in eastern Galicia (western Ukraine) to Canada in 1898. Michael grew up on the homestead farm, completing elementary school there. He had no particular training in carpentry or construction prior to meeting Philip Ruh in the late 1920s when Ruh was designing and constructing the "prairie cathedral" in Mountain Road.

Sawchuk began his association with Ruh in Mountain Road, and followed him to Portage la Prairie in 1928 to assist in the construction of the "prairie cathedral" there. In Portage la Prairie he married Rose Hewko, and lived in that town for many years. From there he travelled with his team – Ruh, Yanchynski and Sawchuk – wherever Ruh had a church to build.

During the 1940s, the building of Ukrainian churches slowed down, and Sawchuk began working for the CNR as a carman-carpenter; he worked there until 1965 when he retired. During these years he continued to be available to Ruh and Yanchynski, as part of a "holy trinity" of builders of Ukrainian churches throughout Canada. He learned his craft from Ruh, whom he admired greatly, not only for his architectural ability, but also for the quality of his religious leadership. As it was with other master builders of Ukrainian churches, Sawchuk's work was largely a "labour of love," for he received only low wages and perhaps room and board from the parish while working on a project. He continued to be a church builder after Ruh's death, constructing his last church-related structure, the new bell tower in Cooks Creek, Manitoba, in the 1960s.

He was a fine craftsman, and he took pride in his work, gaining a reputation in the Ukrainian Catholic community for his dedicated, responsible work. He died in 1972 and is buried with his closest associates, Ruh and Yanchynski, in Cooks Creek.

Michael Swystun
Michael Swystun [fig. 7.9] is one of the few Canadian-born church builders of Ukrainian churches. He was born in a sod dugout (*buda*) on a farm in Oakburn, Manitoba. Later in his life he oversaw the construction of a replica of his birthplace, which still stands today on the family's land. He lived in the Oakburn area all

7.9 Michael Swystun, builder (courtesy M. Swystun estate)

7.10 Michael Tychaliz, builder (courtesy M. Bernat)

his life except for a brief time when he worked for a travelling circus, where he would lift and pull huge masses, often with his teeth. This period of his life was featured in a film entitled "The Strongest Man in the World." Much less is known about his work as a master builder. He is said to have built six churches in Manitoba in the area south of Riding Mountain National Park, the Seech and Solsgirth churches among them. He obtained his only training for church building from his father, who had been a carpenter by trade.

Michael Tychaliz

Born in Hleshchava, Terebovlia, in Galicia in the 1870s, Michael Tychaliz [fig. 7.10] came to Canada shortly after the First World War. He settled in the Dauphin region, where he built several churches, houses and other buildings for local pioneers. He had no formal training in building but had completed village-level schooling and had experience working with builders in Galicia prior to his immigration to Canada. He is known to have built churches in Keld and Kosiw, Manitoba. Friends remember him as a serious, learned and kindly man who was an active member of the Keld Ukrainian cultural community. He was paid very little for his work as master builder but, like other builders of churches, was helped in his endeavours by friends, relatives and neighbours.

Michael Yanchynski

Michael Yanchynski [fig. 7.11] was born on March 18, 1897, in Bukovyna, now in western Ukraine. His parents died when he was very young; he was raised by his grandparents until the age of eight, and after that by neighbours in his village. He received very little formal education, but had become a carpenter by the time he arrived in Canada in 1926 at the age of twenty-eight. He lived first in Portage la Prairie with the people who sponsored his immigration to Canada. There he met the people most important in his life and work thereafter: his wife Mary; Fr. Philip Ruh, who was there building the Church of the Assumption; and Mike

7.11 **Michael Yanchynski, ca. 1935**
(courtesy P. Ruh Collection UCEC)

Sawchuk, who became his close friend and colleague. This team (Mike Yanchynski, his wife Mary, Mike Sawchuk and Fr. Ruh) was responsible for the construction of a great number of Ukrainian churches in Manitoba and elsewhere in Canada.

Yanchynski learned his skills in church building from Fr. Ruh, assisting him in the Portage la Prairie project, and the ones at Cooks Creek and Mountain Road. His first major solo project was the building of the Dauphin church from plans drawn by Fr. Ruh. During his productive years – the 1930s and 1940s – he frequently worked with other builders, such as Mike Sawchuk and Victor Garbet, another of Ruh's assistants. However, he often executed Ruh's designs on his own. Besides building churches, he became proficient at building and finishing copper church domes. Because of his association with Ruh, he was hired to build churches in Ontario, Saskatchewan and Alberta.

In 1950, Yanchynski suffered a tragic accident during the building of the church in Oakburn. While using an electric saw, he lost three fingers at the knuckles on his right hand, and damaged the thumb and remaining finger as well. For many years he could not work at his chosen trade and therefore suffered a significant financial setback. He and his wife made their living from their farm at Cooks Creek, and from the wages she earned in part-time work for Fr. Ruh and at a nearby country club. After his accident, Yanchynski did very little church building. His last project was the construction of the bell tower at Cooks Creek in 1963. He died in 1974 and is buried in Cooks Creek beside his mentor, Fr. Philip Ruh, and his friend Michael Sawchuk, in the cemetery of the church all three of them had helped to build.

Like so many others who worked at the construction and ornamentation of Ukrainian churches in Manitoba, Michael Yanchynski had not been paid justly for his work. In the 1930s, the rate he received was twenty-five cents per hour, in the 1940s he received forty-five cents per hour, and in the 1950s he received two dollars an hour. In the last decade of his life, he worked on church projects for nothing.

Yanchynski is remembered – especially in Cooks Creek – as a generous, intelligent and energetic man who gave much to Ukrainian church building in Manitoba.

ARTISTS

Theodore Baran

Theodore Baran [fig. 7.12] is one of Canada's best-known and respected Ukrainian church artists. He is a painter of icons, murals, church interiors and iconostases, and his work in Manitoba and elsewhere is greatly admired.

Baran was born in western Ukraine in 1910. He completed secondary school in the classical gymnasium of Drohobych, then attended law school in L'viv for two years. However, he soon turned to art, training for four years in L'viv under Professor Julian Pankevych, and for one year in a Ukrainian Catholic Studite monastery in Univ, where he received specialized training in ecclesiastical art. There he studied the Byzantine style, symbolism, and the iconographic and fresco techniques that form the basis of his work in Canadian churches. Before the Second World War, he had already painted churches, one of which was the large Catholic church in Stanyslaviv (present-day Ivano-Frankivske) in 1936. During the war he taught languages and art, and from 1945 to 1949 he was the administrator of a displaced persons camp in Winzer, Germany. He immigrated to Canada in 1949 with his family and settled in Saskatoon, Saskatchewan, where he has lived ever since.

7.12 **Theodore Baran, artist**
(courtesy T. Baran)

His work as an artist began relatively soon after his arrival in Canada. His first commissions were in Saskatchewan, but soon there were a few in Manitoba, particularly in Dauphin [figs. 7.13, 7.14, 7.15] and Oakburn in the 1950s. By 1987, he had painted more than seventy Ukrainian churches, more than fifty of these in Canada and the United States.

Although Baran has painted many church interiors, his major contribution is the fine icon and mural painting he has done. The style, symbols and technique he uses are similar in all his work; yet each completed church has a unique appearance. Decisions about the basic design of the interiors and which icons would be used are always made in consultation with the parish authorities. The preliminary work of erecting scaffolding and preparing the walls is done by hired helpers. The painting of the icons and murals, however, has always been his own work (with occasional help from one of his daughters, Christina).

The uniqueness of Baran's work is expressed in a number of ways: his use of gold-leaf background for his icons and murals; the choice of harmonious and vibrant colours (blues are a favourite); the integration into his paintings of Canadian elements as well as those drawn from traditional Ukrainian church art; and the overall effect of peace and reverence that his work brings to the churches he has painted.

Rather than paint murals directly onto the walls of the church, Baran prefers to paint his icons on canvas or masonite surfaces that can be moved if necessary. He uses special oil paints for the images and twenty-three-karat gold paint for backgrounds.

Baran works alone at home or on location, as circumstances require. He is a man of deep faith and enormous artistic talent. He has always been appreciative of his Ukrainian national traditions, family ties and Canadian homeland. At the age of seventy-six he continues to paint on commission, doing mainly church icons and murals. He also paints portraits, landscapes, still-lives and icons for young couples' traditional wedding ceremonies.

7.13 General view of the interior space of the Church of the Resurrection, Dauphin;
Theodore Baran, artist.

7.14 Deisis, fresco over the altar, Church of the Resurrection, Dauphin; Theodore Baran, artist.

7.15 Frescoes in the dome, Church of the Resurrection, Dauphin; Theodore Baran, artist.

Iconography is an ancient and rare art, one of the oldest styles of painting, and one not familiar to most modern artists. Theodore Baran is one of the foremost living exponents of this art in Canada. Many Ukrainian parishes in Manitoba have had the foresight to have invited Baran to ornament their churches in this very special way.

Dmytro Bartoshuk

Dmytro Bartoshuk [fig. 7.16] was born on February 11, 1910, into a family of seven children in Volhynia. In his youth he was a student at the famous Pochaiv Lavra school, where he studied church painting for four years. His interest in church painting began very early, in fact when he was in the third grade at school. After completing his education and obligatory army service, he painted icons and church interiors in Volhynia. He immigrated to Canada in 1950. His first residence was in Arran, Saskatchewan, where his talent was soon recognized by local people, and he was commissioned to paint icons for a church in Yorkton. He lived in Saskatchewan for a year before moving to

7.16 **Dmytro Bartoshuk**, iconographer (courtesy D. Bartoshuk)

Winnipeg. His hope of getting well-paying work at church painting did not materialize. Instead, from 1951 onward, he worked for Dominion Tannery, then at ordinary house painting. Later, when his health was affected by house painting, he worked for a time as a section man for the CNR. During these years he worked at home in his spare time painting icons, epitaphions (*plashchenytsia*), and making miters for bishops. He also painted church art in other parts of Canada during the course of his life [figs. 7.17, 7.18].

7.17 Icon of Sts. Anthony and Theodosius, St. Mary the Protectress Cathedral, Winnipeg; Dmytro Bartoshuk, iconographer.

7.18 Icon of St. Mark the Evangelist, St. Mary the Protectress Cathedral, Winnipeg; Dmytro Bartoshuk, iconographer.

Bartoshuk had come to Canada with a professional background. However, in the Canadian experience, he was confronted with the problem of poor parishes, the lack of appreciation by some of the clergy for his talent, and his own relative poverty. Nevertheless, he did receive some recognition. He is currently a member of the Standards Committee, which monitors the quality of decoration of Ukrainian Orthodox churches. He has a profound respect for and knowledge of the history and meaning of religion and iconography. He sees icons as images of the eternal, and believes that the painting of icons requires knowledge and understanding of their place in the religious experience. Although he was born and trained in the Ukrainian Orthodox tradition, he is also well-informed about realist iconography in the Western style. He is retired from full-time work and resides in Winnipeg; he continues to do icons on commission.

7.19 Sviatoslav Hordynski, iconographer (courtesy UCEC)

Sviatoslav Hordynski

Sviatoslav Hordynski [fig. 7.19] is a name long associated with the finest in Ukrainian art and literature. Sviatoslav Hordynski was born in 1907, one of four talented children of a scholar of Slavic literature at the University of L'viv. He studied fine arts in Paris and learned several languages. He travelled extensively throughout Ukraine, Russia, Greece and Italy, studying Byzantine art. He became known as a writer of poetry and other literary works long before his emigration to the United States, where he has resided since the Second World War. Although he has suffered from a

7.20 Iconostasis, St. Mary the Protectress Cathedral, Winnipeg; Sviatoslav Hordynski, iconographer.

7.21 Fresco of St. Mary the Protectress on ceiling of nave, St. Mary the Protectress Cathedral, Winnipeg; Sviatoslav Hordynski, iconographer.

hearing handicap for many years, his curiosity, prodigious memory and knowledge of languages have served to provide him with a wealth of knowledge about Ukrainian history and artistic heritage. His particular passion is the revival of the Byzantine tradition in Ukrainian iconography. He has studied and written about the content and technique of this tradition, and some of his works on the subject – and especially on modern iconographers – are standard references.

After emigrating to the United States, Hordynski became more involved in the actual painting of icons. He was commissioned in the 1960s and 1970s to decorate several churches in Manitoba, the most important being the Ukrainian Catholic Cathedral of Sts. Vladimir and Olga in Winnipeg. He worked on that church together with Leo Mol. Hordynski's work has also adorned churches in other parts of Canada and Europe. The other two Manitoba churches that contain his work are the St. Mary the Protectress Orthodox Church [figs. 7.20, 7.21] and the Holy Eucharist Ukrainian Catholic Church, both in Winnipeg.

Hordynski is an exacting craftsman as well as an accomplished artist and researcher. He demands the highest quality of work from all those who work with him. While he is involved with a parish, he is attentive to the requests of his clients, but it is not unusual for him to spend time teaching his clients through lectures and discussions about the intricacy, beauty and background of the art he produces. He is also very open to other developing artists, and almost all the church artists

7.22 Roman Kowal, artist (courtesy R. Kowal)

7.23 Stained-glass window, St. Andrew's Church, Winnipeg; Roman Kowal, artist (courtesy R. Kowal).

who have worked in Manitoba in recent decades attribute much of their inspiration to his example. He is known as a likeable, erudite individual who possesses impressive memory and creativity.

Hordynski continues to work at both his art and writing, despite his advanced age. His written work not only adds to the knowledge about Ukrainian history and culture, but also challenges Soviet percep-

7.24 Mosaic in apse, St. Michael's Church, Winnipeg (Transcona); Roman Kowal, artist (courtesy R. Kowal).

7.25 Jacob Maydanyk in his store, Providence Church Goods, Winnipeg (courtesy UCEC).

tions of this history and culture. His artwork is acclaimed for its vibrancy of colours, faithfulness to the Byzantine tradition, and the attention to precise detail. Hordynski is the author of the authoritative volume on Ukrainian icons entitled *The Ukrainian Icon of the Twelfth to Eighteenth Centuries*, published in 1973.

Roman Kowal

Roman Kowal [fig. 7.22] was born in Ukraine in 1922 and studied art at the Institute of Art in L'viv, Ukraine, and in Germany. In Canada, after 1948, he continued his study of painting, sculpture, mosaics and stained glass. He has maintained a studio in Winnipeg since 1956, where he paints canvasses and does sculptures.

Kowal has done bas-reliefs of major Ukrainian Catholic hierarchs, including Bishop Budka and Archbishop Ladyka. He has painted icons, murals and church interiors as well as stained-glass windows [fig. 7.23] for several churches in Manitoba. Recently Kowal has completed a series of mosaics of the fourteen stations of the cross and the apse for St. Michael's Ukrainian Catholic Church in Transcona [fig. 7.24] and the apse and two major wall mosaics for Holy Family Ukrainian Catholic Church in Winnipeg. In addition, he has completed major works in Alberta and Saskatchewan. In 1984 he completed the monument to the victims of the Ukrainian famine, which stands in front of the Winnipeg City Hall.

Jacob Maydanyk

Jacob Maydanyk [fig. 7.25] contributed to the life of the Ukrainian community in Manitoba and Canada in a variety of ways, one of which was the painting of interiors and icons in Ukrainian churches.

Maydanyk was born in 1891 in Chortkiv county in eastern Galicia (western Ukraine). He completed village school, then went on to the large town of Kolomyia for his secondary schooling. After completing gymnasium (classical high school) there, he studied art in a special school of design near Cracow. He apprenticed with an artist who painted church interiors, meanwhile saving money to go to Canada. He immigrated in 1911, and hoped to earn enough money here to fund art studies in Paris. Arriving in Canada at the age of nineteen, he worked first as a labourer on the railway, and then as a farm hand. In the fall of 1911 he was accepted into the Ruthenian Training School for Teachers in Brandon, Manitoba. There he began to utilize some of his artistic talents, producing cartoon serials based on the character Vooiko Shteef Tabachniuk [fig. 7.26]; the series was a satire on the life of the Ukrainian immigrant labourer in Canada. After completing teacher's college in 1914, he taught in bilingual schools in Oakburn and later Gimli, where there were many Ukrainian settlers. Simultaneously, he did secular and religious art work, cartooning, writing short stories and dramas, and generally becoming involved in the burgeoning cultural and religious activities of Ukrainians in Manitoba.

The outbreak of war in 1914 postponed his hopes for art school in France. Instead he took employment with a French religious goods store, later establishing in Winnipeg his own store, called Providence Church Goods, on Main Street near the CPR station. From there he supplied the large number of Ukrainian churches that mushroomed on the prairies with church artifacts, icons and other items of religious art. He arranged, through his wide contacts in the Canadian West, for the painting of interiors of churches and icons, by hiring budding artists. He developed around himself a group of such apprentices [fig. 7.27], some of whom later became individually known for their work. Among the painters who worked with him were Olga Moroz, Leo Mol and Theodore Baran. Maydanyk continued to do painting of his own, both secular and religious, but continued with his business and serving as intermediary

КАНАДІЙСЬКИЙ УКРАЇНЕЦЬ
ДОДАТОК
ВУЙКО

7.26 Masthead of *Vooiko*, edited and published by Jacob Maydanyk, 1928 (courtesy UCEC).

7.27 Maydanyk workshop at Providence Church Goods, Winnipeg (courtesy UCEC).

between Ukrainian congregations and artists for decoration of their churches.

The artistic style in which he painted was representational, copied from holy pictures to which he had access. Although documentation of his work is scarce, his name is associated with many Ukrainian churches in western Canada built in the 1920s and 1930s.

Maydanyk is remembered as a man of some learning and intelligence, and considerable humour, who was reserved but interested in the world around him, a ready listener and companion for many in the Ukrainian community until his death in 1984. A film entitled "Laughter in my Soul," which focusses on his work as a humourist-cartoonist, was produced by Halya Kuchmij.

Leo Mol

Leo Mol (Leonid Molodozhanyn) is an accomplished artist whose work in sculpture, painting, stained-glass windows and ceramics is known throughout the world [fig. 7.28].

Mol was born in 1915 in Volhynia in present-day western Ukraine, the only child in the family of a potter. It was at home that he had his first exposure to the arts that he would later master. He studied art in Vienna, at the Kunstakademie in Berlin and at the Academy of Art in the Hague, Holland. In Holland, he had his own ceramics business, and also learned the art of making stained glass. He met the woman who later became his wife there, and in 1948 they immigrated to Canada together.

His first years in Winnipeg, where he

**7.28 Leo Mol, artist
(courtesy Andrew Ulicki, Towne Studios Ltd.)**

settled, were times of exploration of opportunities and of his own potential as an artist. He worked first as a farm labourer, then as an employee of Jacob Maydanyk as a painter of icons and church interiors in Manitoba. He continued making and selling pottery and figurines in his home studio. In the early 1950s he was commissioned to do stained-glass windows for the Anglican Church of St. Jude in Winnipeg, and soon other commissions followed. In Manitoba too, he found a type of clay that permitted him to work on the art for which he had been trained – sculpture. In 1953 he entered a competition for the creation of a statue of Sir Robert Borden in Ottawa; he was one of the six prize winners. Throughout the 1950s he developed his skills as a sculptor, simultaneously earning a reputation as a master in stained-glass window technique. Altogether, some eighty stained-glass windows in Winnipeg are by Mol.

In 1964, Mol reached a turning point in his life: he entered and won a competition for the creation of a statue of Taras Shevchenko, which was to be erected in Washington, D.C. Together with Ukrainian architect Radoslav Zuk of Montreal, he created the monument to Shevchenko – a fourteen-foot bronze statue on a square on Embassy Row. This was the first of many impressive sculptures that were created by Mol, among them many portrait busts of the world's leading political and religious figures, as well as nudes. A recent commission was for the creation of a sculpture of John Diefenbaker on the grounds of the House of Commons.

Mol is considered by experts to be a "leading sculptor in the classic tradition," and to demonstrate "a highly sensitive and personal interpretation of the character of each subject," [fig. 7.29] while displaying "considerable

7.29 "Tom Lamb, Pioneer Bush Pilot," civic statue, Winnipeg; Leo Mol, artist.

talent in adjusting his technique to capture the personality of the sitter."[5] Moreover, Mol developed his own foundry in Manitoba so he could use a process which dates from the ninth century B.C. for casting sculptures in bronze. Having the foundry allows him to complete more of his sculptures in Manitoba rather than do them in foundries in Europe and the United States, as he had done previously. A film entitled "Immortal Images," featuring Mol and his technique, was made in the 1960s by Slavko Novitsky for the National Film Board of Canada.

As a sculptor, Mol was more prolific than he was as a Ukrainian church artist, but his religious work was no less impressive. The work in Ukrainian churches in his first years in Manitoba for Jacob Maydanyk included the painting of icons, banners and altar cloths. His most massive and important religious works of art are the sixteen stained-glass windows in Sts. Vladimir and Olga Ukrainian Catholic Cathedral in Winnipeg [fig. 7.30]. These windows portray in rich composition and brilliant jewel colours the events in the history of Christianity and of Ukraine, important Christian holy days, as well as emblems of Ukraine. In these he is said to "vividly show the major events in the history of Christianity in Ukraine."[6] One of his most recent works in this style is the monumental mosaic of the Holy Trinity on the facade of the Holy Trinity Ukrainian Orthodox Cathedral, Winnipeg [fig. 7.31].

Leo Mol is an artist who is thoroughly aware of his tradition, his craft and his place in art and Ukrainian history. He has known, worked with, and painted or sculpted some of the greatest Canadian and Ukrainian art figures – for example, some of the Group of Seven painters, and Sviatoslav Hordynski. He has received many honours, including honorary doctorates, prizes for his work, and recognition from the Ukrainian community and the Canadian government. He lives and works in Winnipeg and continues to be active in the artistic and Ukrainian communities of Manitoba and across Canada. He has done much to advance and accentuate the Ukrainian culture and heritage across this country; he truly is a gift to all Canadians.

7.30   "The Baptism of Princess Olga and Prince Vladimir," stained-glass windows, Sts. Vladimir and Olga Cathedral, Winnipeg; Leo Mol, artist (courtesy L. Mol).

7.31 "The Holy Trinity," mosaic on the monumental facade of the Holy Trinity Cathedral, Winnipeg; Leo Mol, artist (courtesy L. Mol).

Olga Moroz

Olga Moroz (nee Ewanchyn) is one of the few but growing number of women to be a painter of icons and interiors of churches [fig.7.32]. She was born in Ozerna, Manitoba, the eighth of twelve children. Her first professional work as a church painter was for Jacob Maydanyk in Winnipeg, accomplished concurrently with her art studies. Maydanyk passed on to her some of the many commissions he received in the 1930s from Ukrainian churches in Manitoba and elsewhere in Canada. During her work as a church painter, she knew and admired the style and artistic talent of Hnat

7.32 Olga Moroz, iconographer (courtesy O. Moroz)

Sych, although her style differed from his [fig. 7.33]. In 1939 she married Rev. Nicholas Moroz, a Ukrainian Orthodox priest. From then on, she painted churches wherever her husband's work took her. She noted that in those years, although parishes were not wealthy, "churches had to be respected and beautiful," and that "there existed 'Picassos' even in the West of Canada."[7] She followed the principles of the Byzantine style in her painting. After many years doing other types of painting, Moroz started doing church painting again, from her home in British Columbia. She lives in Victoria.

7.33 Icon of The Virgin Mary, Sts. Peter and Paul Church, Seech; Olga Moroz, iconographer.

Vera Senchuk

Vera Senchuk (nee Lazarowich) represents a transitional period in the art of iconography in Ukrainian churches in Manitoba [fig. 7.34]. One of the few women to be involved in this work, she is Canadian born and trained. Her role models and mentors are two of the men who have made a great mark in the field: Sviatoslav Hordynski and Dmytro Bartoshuk. Vera Senchuk was born in Hafford, Saskatchewan, to a family whose father had immigrated to Canada in 1926 and whose mother had arrived after the Second World War. She grew up on a farm, receiving elementary education in the local school, secondary schooling in Saskatoon, and earning a Bachelor of Arts degree in history from the University of Saskatchewan. She had shown artistic talent in her youth and was encouraged by her parents, especially her mother, who was herself a talented folk artist working in embroidery, weaving and Easter-egg painting. Vera Senchuk studied commercial art and some art history, confining her work until about 1980 to Easter-egg painting, conducting art classes, and doing private painting for friends.

7.34 Vera Senchuk, iconographer (courtesy V. Senchuk)

Aware of the long tradition of male artists in Ukrainian and other iconography, she hesitated taking up the painting of icons until she met Dmytro Bartoshuk in Winnipeg in 1981. Encouraged by his example and his praise of her work, she began to paint church icons and banners on commission for the Ukrainian Orthodox Church of Canada's consistory. To date, she has done a number of individual icons and four complete iconostases in western Canada, one of which is in Manitoba [fig. 7.35]. In 1987, she completed a commission for the Ukrainian Women's Association's millennium project in Saskatchewan, which is a series of twelve icons.

7.35 Iconostasis, Holy Trinity Church, Lennard; Vera Senchuk, iconographer (courtesy V. Senchuk).

7.36 **General view of the nave and apse, Church of the Assumption of the Blessed Virgin Mary, Portage la Prairie; Hnat Sych, artist.**

Senchuk tends to be a strict traditionalist in her style, taking her model for icons from the Byzantine period of iconography and adding to them a Ukrainian form. She works in oils, acrylic and egg tempera, depending on the the terms of the commission. She has learned a great deal of her technique from working with Dmytro Bartoshuk, but her style differs from his in important ways. Being a female iconographer, Vera Senchuk could very well be at the forefront of a tradition. She currently lives and works in Winnipeg, Manitoba.

Hnat Sych

Hnat Sych figured prominently among the artists who painted icons and decorated the interiors of churches in Manitoba. He was born in Galicia and is said to have had formal art training in L'viv, the capital of western Ukraine. Sych travelled from his home in Winnipeg to many parts of Manitoba to paint the icons and interiors of churches, as well as the backdrops (*kurtyna*) of stages used for dramatic performances. His most productive time was in the 1920s and the 1930s, when he painted the large, now-demolished Church of the Assumption of the Blessed Virgin Mary in Portage la Prairie [fig. 7.36], the Church of the Holy Eucharist in Rosa, and several others. He was assisted in his work by members of his family (his brother and his son), by acquaintances in the district, and by hired workers. In every situation he acted as general contractor and main designer for the painting of the church. He took on the responsibility of coordinating the purchase and use of the paint, scaffolds and other materials, and also did the bulk of the ornamental painting and iconography.

Many examples of his work have been found, but the history of the man himself is elusive. Probably his most monumental work is the collection of over fifty icons that he painted on the walls of the church in Portage la Prairie. He painted his murals on canvas that was glued to the walls. The marbling effect on the walls and arcades of this church were also his handiwork, and they were a marvel to see. He had a reputation of being exceptionally skilled at moving among scaffolds forty or fifty

7.37 "Moses," oil on canvas, glued to plaster wall, Church of the Assumption of the Blessed Virgin Mary, Portage la Prairie; Hnat Sych, artist.

7.38 "Two Apostles," oil on canvas, glued to plaster wall, in the apse of the Church of the Assumption of the Blessed Virgin Mary, Portage la Prairie; Hnat Sych, artist.

feet above the floor. He had a habit (not unlike that of many painters in earlier times) of painting into his icons the faces of members of the parish, not always in a complimentary manner. For example, he is said to have painted into the icon depicting Hell the face of a parishioner who opposed paying him for his work.

Sych is one of the best-known artists of the 1920s and 1930s, but information about him is far from complete. His artistry has been described as primitive. Yet his work clearly shows that he had some knowledge of traditional religious scenes; whether he obtained his knowledge from holy pictures or prints of icons, however, is unclear. His work also shows that he had a rather modest knowledge of anatomy [fig. 7.37]. In the Portage la Prairie church, there were several paintings with distinctly Canadian features, such as lakes and pine trees in settings that were meant to depict the Holy Land during the life of Christ [fig. 7.38]. On the whole, he was a talented if not formally educated artist who certainly made his mark on Manitoba's Ukrainian church art.

EPILOGUE

OUR INTENTION IN WRITING THIS BOOK was to show the continuity of tradition that links present-day Manitoba Ukrainians to their forebears, who received Christianity on the shores of the Dnieper River a thousand years ago. Having accepted their faith from Byzantium, they very quickly made it their own. Enriching it with their creative genius, they endowed this faith and tradition with a dynamism that permitted it to endure the vicissitudes of countless historic events. Through wars, conquest and subjugation, through good times and through bad, the Ukrainian people maintained their faith and their traditions, which they brought with them to the New World. The churches they built on the prairies attest to their tenacity and their determination to maintain their faith and traditions against all odds. Here, in Manitoba, the builders and the artists who created these churches found the freedom and opportunity to exercise their creative talents.

We trust that the overview presented in this book has helped the reader gain a perspective and a sense of history. We hope that, whenever a reader happens to see Ukrainian churches, with their cupolas and domes, whether they be modest or grand, these churches will truly be appreciated as timeless monuments to the Christian faith and its traditions.

APPENDIX 1:
GUIDE TO UKRAINIAN CHURCHES

THE EXTERIOR

Ukrainian churches appear in several shapes: the form of a cross [figs. A.1, A.2, A.3], the shape of a ship [figs. A.4, A.5], the shape of a star, or the form of a circle.

The cross shape signifies the building's dedication to Christ, who was crucified on a cross to redeem sinners. The shape of the ship shows that it is through the church that believers are saved; the ship is an early Christian symbol of the temptations and tribulations a traveller on a ship (or a believer) undergoes to reach his or her destination.

The star-shaped church in eight angles signifies the star of the East, which led the first wise men. Thus the church is to guide the believer to the Heavenly Kingdom – to salvation. The circular church (an early form of church architecture) reminds the believer that, like the circle, the church is endless and eternal.

The cupola, or dome (*bania*), and its topping with a cross is an important feature of most Ukrainian churches [figs. A.6, A.7, A.8].

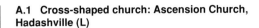

A.1 Cross-shaped church: Ascension Church, Hadashville (L)

A.2 Cross-shaped church: Holy Ascension Church, Ashville (M)

A.3 Cross-shaped church: Holy Ghost Church, Zoria (R)

A.4 The shape of a ship: St. John the Baptist Church, Caliento (L)

A.5 The shape of a ship: Assumption of the Blessed Virgin Mary Church, Ashville (R)

A.6 Protruding domes: Church of the Resurrection, Dauphin (L)

A.7 Wooden-domed church: St. Volodymyr Chapel, Camp Morton (R)

However, today the traditional onion-shaped domes are on occasion being stylized and modernized. The churches can have from one to thirteen cupolas. The single-cupola church has a large cupola in the centre [fig. A.9]. The three-cupola church has a central dome with two smaller domes usually in the front [figs. A.10, A.11]. The five-cupola church has a dominant dome in the centre and four smaller domes around it [fig. A.12]. Other variants, of three, seven, nine and thirteen cupolas, also exist [fig. A.13].

A.8 Cross-topped dome: St. John the Baptist Church, Caliento (L)

A.9 Single-domed church: Holy Eucharist Church, Oakburn (R)

A.10 Three-domed church: St. Mary the Protectress Church, Selo Ukraina (L)

A.11 Three-domed church: Holy Spirit Church, Lennard (R)

A.12 Five-domed church (view from the back; the two front domes are not visible): Church of the Resurrection, Dauphin (L)

A.13 Seven-domed church: Immaculate Conception Church, Cooks Creek (R)

The single cupola represents Christ. The three cupolas represent the Trinity. Five cupolas represent Christ and the four evangelists. Seven cupolas represent the seven gifts of the Holy Spirit. Nine represent the nine ranks of the angelic world. Thirteen cupolas represent Christ and the twelve apostles.

The windows of Ukrainian churches are usually made of clear glass [figs. A.14, A.15]. However, in Canada, when available, coloured glass has been introduced, often in conjuction with single-bar or triple-bar cross motifs [fig. A.16]. Some Ukrainian church designers have recently introduced stained-glass windows featuring iconographic ornamentation [figs. A.17, A.18].

Ukrainian churches sometimes have mosaic frescoes on their front exterior walls that also feature iconographic themes.

THE INTERIOR

Upon entering a Ukrainian church, one is struck by the richly decorated interior, the multi-coloured icons, and an impressive icon screen wall known as the iconostasis. The interiors of all Ukrainian churches have a certain set pattern guided by the tradition of Eastern Christianity and based on the Byzantine liturgical rite.

The Three Areas
Ukrainian church interiors are usually divided into three parts: the sanctuary, the nave and the narthex. The sanctuary (always elevated) and the nave are separated by the iconostasis. The narthex is usually the entrance area of the church. The nave and the narthex are not always formally separated.

The church's three parts are based on the plan of the Old Testament tabernacle of Moses and the Temple of Solomon. St. Symeon the

142

A.14 Plain stock windows, interior view, Blessed Virgin Mary Church, St. Norbert (L)

A.15 Plain stock windows (exterior view), Holy Trinity Church, Stuartburn (R)

A.16 Windows symbolizing cross, St. George's Church, Dauphin (L)

A.17 Stained-glass window in arch, St. Nicholas Church, Winnipeg (R)

A.18 Stained-glass windows with iconographic depiction and Ukrainian motifs, Sts. Vladimir and Olga Cathedral, Winnipeg

New Theologian (957 – 1022), a prominent writer on theology and liturgy, refers to this tripartition as a reminder of: either the Trinity; the three orders of celestial hierarchs; or the Christian people divided into three categories (the clergy, the faithful and the catechumens).

The sanctuary [figs. A.19, A.20] is the most important part of the church and is reserved for the clergy and male faithful (the sacristan, sub-deacons and altar boys). Here the sacrament of Eucharist is celebrated on the altar. The sanctuary is in the eastern part of the building, which itself faces east. In the sanctuary there are two major tables, the altar (*prestil*) at the centre, and the table of oblation (*zhertivnyk*) at the wall on the left side of the sanctuary. Both of these tables have very important liturgical functions during the holy liturgy. The half-rounded rear wall of the sanctuary is called the apse; it is traditionally painted with icons according to a specific plan [figs. A.21, A.22, A.23].

A.19 Interior view of church looking towards the sanctuary, St. Volodymyr Chapel, Camp Morton (L)

A.20 Interior view of church looking towards the iconostasis, Holy Trinity Church, Vita (R)

A.21 Interior view facing the sanctuary (note the statues on the left and right sides of the apse), Holy Ghost Church, Zoria (L)

A.22 View of the apse in a church without iconostasis, Immaculate Conception Church, Cooks Creek (R)

A.23 Interior view, facing the sanctuary, of a church without iconostasis, Holy Eucharist Church, Oakburn (L)

A.24 North wall of a church, Holy Eucharist Church, Oakburn (R)

A.25 South wall of a church, Holy Eucharist Church, Oakburn

The sanctuary corresponds to the holy of the holies of the Old Testament Temple, the most sacred area of the Temple. The orientation eastward is based on two ideas. First, east is identified with sunrise, which will usher in the "eighth day" (the second coming of Christ at the end of the world). Second, east is the direction of Jerusalem – the place where many events in the life of Christ occurred, including His resurrection. The sanctuary thus represents the house of God, the heaven of heavens, or that which goes beyond the created world – that is, the spiritual world.

The nave is the central part of the church, or the church proper, where the congregation gathers for worship. In the older Ukrainian churches in Canada there were no pews, and worshippers stood throughout the liturgy. (There were, however, benches along the walls for the elderly.) Today, in most churches, there are rows of pews [figs. A.24, A.25]. There often is an elevated balcony for the choir and cantor at the west end of the nave.

145

At the easternmost end of the nave, in front of the iconostasis, there is a three- or four-step elevated area, which is known as the solea. This area is utilized for the liturgical processions during the course of the holy liturgy. At the centre of the solea, and usually projected in a half circle, there is the ambo (*amvon*). Here, the priest reads the Gospel, delivers the sermon and dispenses the Eucharist to the believers. The deacon chants the litanies of the liturgy from this area too, facing the royal doors.

The nave corresponds to the "holy area" of the Jewish Temple. The nave represents the created world and, according to St. Maximus the Confessor (580 – 662), "the sanctuary and the nave communicate: the sanctuary enlightens and guides the nave, which becomes its visible expression."

The narthex is the area of the church for those preparing themselves to enter the church (the penitents or the catechumens of the early church). Today few people are penitents or catechumens and thus the narthex has a more practical application. However, it is here that the priest leads in all new-born infants for the sacraments of baptism and chrismation.

The narthex corresponds to the courtyard of the Old Testament Temple; it symbolizes the unredeemed part of the world, that is, the world lying in sin. It is located opposite the sanctuary.

Icons

Some of the most distinctive features of Ukrainian churches are the icons (*ikona* or *obraz*) [figs. A.26, A.27]. Icons abound in Ukrainian churches and are found on the walls, ceiling, domes, the apse and the iconostasis; they are either mounted or framed on them [figs. A.28, A.29, A.30, A.31], or are painted directly on the surfaces. Icons surround the

A.26 Icon of the Mother of God, St. Michael's Church, Winnipeg (Transcona) (L)

A.27 Icon of the Mother of God with sculptured silver (*repoussé*) cladding. Note the embroidered towel that is traditionally wrapped around the icon on three sides. St. Michael's Church, Winnipeg (Transcona). (R)

A.28 Framed paper icon (probably brought from Ukraine), St. Mary the Protectress Church, Selo Ukraina (L)

A.29 Framed icon of the Mother of God, St. Michael's Church, Gardenton (M)

A.30 Framed icon of St. Nicholas, Assumption of the Blessed Virgin Mary Church, Ashville (R)

A.31 Framed icon of St. Michael the Archangel, St. Michael's Church, Winnipeg (Transcona)

Ukrainian believer when he or she worships in the church. Icons are always two dimensional. However, on occasion in Ukrainian Catholic churches under Western influence, statues (three dimensional representations) are seen.

Icons are depictions of sacred persons and scenes from the Old and the New testaments, especially Christ and the Mother of God. Honour, or homage, is paid to them by the Ukrainian believer, and the icons pass the homage on to their prototypes, that is, to the figures depicted on the icons.

The Seventh Ecumenical Council in 787 (held in Nicea) defined the purpose of icons as follows: "The more a person contemplates the icons, the more he or she is reminded of what they represent, the more he or she will be inclined to venerate them, prostrating himself, without, however, evincing toward them the true adoration which belongs to God alone. Whoever venerates an icon venerates the person it represents."

The Iconographic Scheme in the Sanctuary and Nave
The icons in a Ukrainian church are positioned according to a definite scheme that is rooted in theological considerations. At the lowest level are found the Church Fathers, who are usually the people that composed the liturgy. Also found here are the hierarchs, or deacons, of the early Christian Church.

The two major liturgies celebrated are those of St. John Chrysostom and St. Basil the Great. These saints, along with other fourth- and fifth-century saints, are usually depicted at the lowest level.

Above and immediately behind the altar is found the Eucharist scene: Christ dispensing communion to the apostles in the form of bread and wine.

The dispensing of the Eucharist at every liturgy symbolizes Christ's dispensing of it at the Last Supper.

The icon of the Mother of God in the oranta position (hands outstretched and uplifted) is found on the third level.

The Mother of God personifies the Church itself, because She contained in Herself the Creator of the world. The oranta position is one of prayer and indicates the completeness of the sacrifice. The priest uses this same gesture during the Eucharistic canon of the liturgy.

On the fourth level is found the icon of Christ.

The icon of Christ shows that Christ is Himself the offered sacrifice and the sanctifier who offers.

The icon of Pentecost is usually found on the highest vaults of the sanctuary.

The Pentecost feast is represented because it symbolizes the Holy Spirit as sanctifier of the Church and of the Eucharist.

In many Ukrainian churches in Canada, the apse is decorated with only some of the five levels, and variants of the traditional iconographic scheme of the apse in the sanctuary are not uncommon [figs. A.32, A.33].

The icons are placed according to special schemes in the nave as well. The central dome is the traditional location of the figure of Christ Pantocrator. Many Ukrainian churches have their main chandelier hanging from the centre of the dome and therefore may not feature the icon of the Pantocrator; the dome is then depicted as the celestial world [figs. A.34, A.35, A.36] with five- and six-pointed stars. Below the icon of

Christ Pantocrator in the dome are depicted the prophets and apostles, particularly those who announced and established the Church. The four evangelists are ususally found in the four corners, or pendentives [fig. A.37]. Between the dome and the eye-level area of the nave, the pillars, walls and columns are decorated with the figures of martyrs, saints and ascetics. Sometimes there are scenes from the New Testament on the walls, pertaining especially to the major feasts of the Church. On the west wall is the depiction of the Last Judgement. Thus, upon leaving the church, the believer is reminded of the fundamental Christian truth of the Last Judgement. The narthex is not usually embellished with icons.

The icon of Christ Pantocrator shows Christ as Judge with arms outstretched, blessing with the right hand. Usually in the left hand He holds an open Gospel bearing John's quote, "I am the way, and the truth, and the light."

A.32   Frescoes in the apse, Church of the Resurrection, Dauphin (L)

A.33   Detail of fresco depicting St. Mary the Protectress, in apse, Church of the Resurrection, Dauphin (R)

A.34   The celestial world depicted in the main dome, Church of the Resurrection, Dauphin (L)

A.35   The celestial world depicted in the main dome, Holy Eucharist Church, Oakburn (R)

The evangelists announced the good news about Christ to the world. Also they preached the universal message of the Gospel to the four parts of the world.

The Last Judgement symbolizes the end of church history and the beginning of the age that is to come. In the Creed, the final verse states: "I look for the resurrection of the dead and the Life of the world to come."

A.36   The celestial world with angels in the dome, Holy Ghost Church, Zoria

A.37   The four evangelists in the pendentive of a dome, Immaculate Conception Church, Cooks Creek: (a) St. Matthew; (b) St. Luke;

(c) St. John; (d) St. Mark.

Throughout most Ukrainian churches, the icons are interspersed with geometric patterns known as *rospys* [fig. A.38], usually based on folk designs and embroidery, or Christian symbols (the stylized cross or the anchor, for example).

A.38 Floral geometric designs (*rospys*) on the walls of the Assumption of the Blessed Virgin Mary Church, Ashville

The Iconostasis

The most unusual feature of Ukrainian churches is the iconostasis, which is an icon-bearing wall or screen separating the sanctuary from the nave [figs. A.39, A.40, A.41, A.42, A.43]. It consists of up to four tiers of icons arranged according to a prescribed scheme. The smaller churches often have only the first two tiers. There are three doors in the lower tier of the iconostasis, which provide accesses to the altar area.

> According to the Fathers of the Church, the iconostasis symbolizes the boundary between two worlds: divine and human, permanent and transitory. Not only does the iconostasis separate the two worlds, but at the same time it unites them. By means of the icons, the believer is led to contemplate the reconciliation of the two worlds, at the "end of time."

The central doors, known as the royal doors, or the holy doors (*tsars'ki dveri*), are double doors that open inwards. There are prescribed liturgical times when the royal doors are opened or closed by the bishop, the priest or the deacon, who are the only orders permitted to use them. The doors bear circular icons of the four evangelists, which are best seen when the doors are closed. The upper parts of the doors bear the icon of the Annunciation, which is divided into two along the opening between the doors (the angel is found on one and the Mother of God on the other). In addition, the doors are often richly carved with vines and leaves [figs. A.44, A.45].

A.39 One-level iconostasis, St. John the Baptist Church, Caliento (L)

A.40 One-level iconostasis, Holy Ghost Church, Beausejour (R)

A.41 One-level iconostasis, St. Demetrius Church, Malonton (moved to Camp Veselka, near Gimli) (L)

A.42 Three-level iconostasis, St. Mary the Protectress Cathedral, Winnipeg (R)

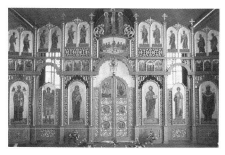

A.43 Three-level iconostasis, Holy Spirit Church, Lennard (L)

A.44 The royal doors of the iconostasis, St. Mary the Protectress Cathedral, Winnipeg (M)

A.45 Detail of royal doors, showing the four evangelists, St. John the Baptist Church, Caliento (R)

153

The royal doors are so named because during the liturgy the priests carrying the holy sacrament of the Eucharist enter through them to place the gifts on the altar. The Heavenly King Himself enters through these doors and sanctifies all believers who participate in the Eucharist.

The four evangelists are witness to the presence of Christ's good news: the Gospel of Salvation.

The annunciation was the first proclamation to the world of the Gospel.

The deacons' doors (*dyiakons'ki dveri*), located to the right and the left of the royal doors, are utilized by deacons and minor orders such as sub-deacons, sacristans and and altar boys [figs. A.46, A.47]. The deacons' doors have icons on them that depict either the early deacons of the Church (e.g., St. Stephen) or archangels (usually Gabriel and Michael). The one on the left is commonly called the north door and the one on the right is known as the south door.

A.46 Deacons' doors, St. John the Baptist Church, Caliento: (a) left or "north" door; (b) right or "south" door. (L)

A.47 Deacons' doors, St. Mary the Protectress Cathedral, Winnipeg: (a) St. Stephen; (b) Archangel Michael. (R)

The first tier of the iconostasis also bears a number of traditionally prescribed icons. Looking directly at the iconostasis, one sees the icon of Christ [fig. A.48] to the right of the royal doors, and the icon of the Mother of God and Christ Child [fig. A.49] to the left. The space to the right of the south deacons' door is usually reserved for the icon of the patron saint or feast day of the parish [fig. A.50]. The space to the left of the north deacon's door is usually reserved for the icon of some prominent saint, such as, for example, St. John the Baptist or St. Nicholas [fig. A.51].

Symbolically, the two icons – of Christ and the Mother of God – show that everything that happens to the believer happens in history, that is, between two events – the two comings of Christ: the first as the Saviour born of Mary, and the second at the end of time, when Christ will come as King and Judge.

A.48   Icon of Christ on iconostasis, St. Mary the Protectress Cathedral, Winnipeg (far L)

A.49   Icon of the Mother of God, St. Mary the Protectress Cathedral, Winnipeg (L)

A.50   Patron saint icon, St. Mary the Protectress, on iconostasis, St. Mary the Protectress Cathedral, Winnipeg. Note the "protecting veil" (*pokrova*) held by the Virgin Mary. (R)

A.51   Icon of St. Nicholas on iconostasis, St. Mary the Protectress Cathedral, Winnipeg (far R)

The second tier usually contains a series of smaller icons dedicated to the twelve major feast days of the Church [fig. A.52]. Here also, above the royal doors, is found an icon of the Mystical Supper [fig. A.53] showing Christ and his apostles at the Last Supper.

The Twelve Feasts depict principal stages of the action of Divine Providence in the world.

The third row of icons shows two groups of six apostles [fig. A.54], each usually facing the centre icon (the deisis): Christ enthroned with the Mother of God on His right and St. John the Baptist on His left.

The twelve apostles are the bearers of the "good news" to the universe.

The term *deisis* means prayer. The two figures are standing in prayer before Christ the Saviour.

Sometimes a fourth row is found, consisting of two sets of Old Testament forefathers, patriarchs and prophets also facing the centre icon (the Mother of God holding the Christ Child).

The patriarchs and prophets facing the centre icon are symbolic of the idea that the prophets foretold that the Mother of God was to bear the Saviour Christ. The prophets have in their hands open scrolls depicting their prophecies. The patriarchs represent the carnal ancestors of Christ.

At the top of the iconostasis is usually found the Cross of Golgotha with Christ on it, and on either side are the figures of the Mother of God and St. John the Evangelist [fig. A.55]. The entire iconostasis is decorated with various carved ornaments with floral, animal, tree, fruit and bird motifs.

A.52 Icon of three major feast days (second level of iconostasis). From left to right, the Resurrection, the Dormition of the Mother of God, and the Transfiguration. St. Mary the Protectress Cathedral, Winnipeg. (L)

A.53 The Mystical Supper (second level of the iconostasis), St. Mary the Protectress Cathedral, Winnipeg (R)

A.54 Detail of icons of the Apostles (third level of the iconostasis): (a) St. John and St. Philip; (b) St. Thomas and St. Bartholomew. St. Mary the Protectress Cathedral, Winnipeg. (L) (M)

A.55 Christ crucified with the Mother of God and St. John (top of the central part of the iconostasis), St. Mary the Protectress Cathedral, Winnipeg (R)

The floral, animal, tree, fruit and bird motifs are symbolic of Paradise and express the need of all believers to prepare themselves for the Final Judgement.

Many churches have splendidly carved iconostases, and Manitoba has many rich examples. There are numerous variations on the traditional composition of the iconostasis [fig. A.56], but all of them have a rhythmic arrangement and are highly symmetrical.

The Holy Tables
In the Ukrainian Church there are three special tables, which play important roles in church services: the altar, the table of oblation and the tetrapod.

The altar (*prestil*) is the most important and central part of the entire church building [figs. A.57, A.58]. It is here that the bread and wine are mystically transformed into the body and blood of Christ in the sacrament of the Eucharist. Only ordained individuals are admitted to celebrate before the altar. The altar table is made of wood or stone and takes the form of a free-standing cube. In the early Church, church buildings stood on the sites of the burial places of martyrs and saints. Relics of saints are placed in the bottom of the altar when both altar and church are being consecrated. The altar is covered with two layers of rich cloth.

A.56   Detail of iconostasis wood carving, Church of the Holy Eucharist, Rosa

The altar represents the mystical presence of the heavenly throne and table of the Kingdom of God. It is the table of Christ the Word, both Lamb and King, with dominion over all creation.

The relics remind the faithful that the Church was established on the blood of martyrs.

The rich cloth that covers the altar signifies the altar's divine and heavenly character.

On the altar are placed seven liturgical items. One is the tabernacle [fig. A.59], a small church-shaped container, found toward the back central half of the altar. Sometimes it is a miniature of the church building itself. Here are kept the eucharistic gifts for the sick, which are prepared on Holy Thursday of each year. Also found on the altar is the seven-branched candelabra [figs. A.60, A.61], placed behind the tabernacle.

The seven-branched candelabra has its origins in Jewish Temple worship. It symbolizes the Lord's illumination of the world with His spiritual light. The number seven is a popular sacred number in Eastern Christianity, along with 3, 12, 40 and 50.

The antimension is also found on the altar. It is a rectangular silk or linen cloth on which is the depiction of the icon of Christ in the tomb. The antimension also has on it the printed images of the four evangelists in the corners, as well as the signature of the ruling bishop. Into one of the corners of the antimension is inserted a relic of a saint. The antimension is always folded, and only during the course of a liturgy is it unfolded on the altar, for on it will be placed the holy gifts of the

A.57 Altar in Sts. Volodymyr and Olha Church, Gilbert Plains (L)

A.58 Altar in Holy Eucharist Church, Oakburn (R)

A.59 Tabernacle on altar, Blessed Virgin Mary Church, St. Norbert (L)

A.60 Candelabra on altar, St. Michael's Church, Gardenton (M)

A.61 Candelabra in St. Elias Church, Sirko (R)

Eucharist. (No lay person may handle the antimension, but often clergy will gladly show the antimension to visitors).

The signature of the bishop is the sign that the local community has the permission of the bishop to gather at the church.

The use of relics symbolizes the early church practice of celebrating the Eucharist on the site of the burial of martyrs and saints.

A liturgy cannot be celebrated without the antimension.

The fourth item is the iliton, which is a square piece of rich material on which the antimension is placed.

The iliton symbolizes both the swaddling clothes at Christ's birth and the winding sheet at His burial.

The fifth liturgical item found on the altar is the Gospel, which is a richly decorated book whose firm covers are overlaid in gold or silver [figs. A.62, A.63, A.64, A.65]. The covers show in bas-relief the four evangelists in the corners and the risen Christ in the centre. At the

A.62 Gospel book in St. Michael and the Angels Church, Tyndall (L)

A.63 Gospel book from the altar, and smaller Gospel book for visitations outside the church, St. John the Baptist Church, Dry River (R)

beginning of the liturgy the Gospel lies flat on the antimension, but later, after the Small Procession and the reading of the Gospel, it stands elevated on the altar between the tabernacle and the antimension. The Gospel is given much homage in the Ukrainian Church.

The Gospel, or the "Good News," is read at every liturgy and points the way to salvation for believers.

The hand cross is also found on the altar. It is a wooden, silver or gold cross that is utilized by the priest for blessing the congregation. In early Manitoba Ukrainian churches, many of the hand crosses were of finely-carved wood, and were works of art.

The cross reminds the believer that salvation was only achieved through Christ's crucifixion on the cross.

The seventh item is the ciborium (*daronosytsia*), which is a container utilized to bring the Eucharist to the sick and the infirm. The ciborium is usually kept in the tabernacle.

The oblation table is found in the sanctuary to the northeast (far left) of the altar, along the wall of the apse [fig. A.66]. It is at this table that

A.64   Gospel book in Holy Trinity Church, Vita (L)

A.65   Gospel book in St. Michael's Church, Winnipeg (Transcona) (M)

A.66   Oblation tables, Church of the Holy Eucharist, Rosa (R)

the Eucharistic gifts are prepared during the early part of the liturgy, at a service known as the proskomedia. Later in the liturgy, during the Great Entrance Procession, the gifts are brought to the altar. On the wall above the oblation table there is usually an icon of Christ praying in Gethsemane, or of the Nativity.

Christ praying in Gethsemane is the last independent act of Christ before He offered Himself as a sacrifice for all people.

The proskomedia is sometimes thought to represent the birth of Christ in the conceptualization of the liturgy as the unfolding of the life of Christ.

The table of oblation is covered with a fine silk or satin cloth, as is the altar. It is considerably smaller than the altar. It can be seen easily through the north deacons' door. The oblation table supports a number of sacred items utilized during the liturgy.

The chalice [fig. A.67] and the paten (*chasha* and *dyskos*), are the two principal vessels for the Eucharist. The chalice is a goblet of silver or gold, and the paten is a circular, flat plate on a raised stand also made of silver or gold [fig. A.68]. In some churches these two vessels were brought from Ukraine, but today most come from Canada, the United States or Greece. Above the paten is placed the star (also known as the asterisk), which is a double-arched metal band held together at the centre in the form of a cross.

The chalice holds the wine, mixed with water, which later become the communion gifts. It represents the cup used by Christ in the Mystical Supper. The paten holds the specially prepared pieces of bread, known as the prosphora, which later becomes consecrated into the Body of Christ. It represents the manger in which Christ was placed upon His birth. Later in the liturgy, it represents the

A.67   Chalice, Holy Eucharist Church, Oakburn (L)

A.68   Paten with star and chalice, St. John the Baptist Church, Caliento (R)

tomb of Christ. The star is placed on the paten to keep the veil from touching the prepared pieces of prosphora. The star symbolizes the star of Bethlehem, which shone in the sky when Christ was born.

Two veils made of silk or satin cover the chalice and paten. They are sewn in the shape of a cross with a central fixed part.

The veils covering the chalice and paten are symbolic of the swaddling clothes in which Christ was wrapped after His birth.

The aer is a third veil, a large, rectangular piece of silk or satin, which covers both the chalice and paten with their smaller veils.

The aer is symbolic of the winding sheet (the shroud) with which the body of Christ was wrapped for burial.

The spoon and the spear are two instruments made of gold or silver, which are also found on the table of oblation. The spoon is used to dispense the Eucharist to the worshipper, while the spear is used in the preparation of the bread (prosphora), which is placed on the paten.

The spear is symbolic of the one used to pierce the side of Christ during His passion on the cross.

Two candlesticks usually stand at the rear two corners of the oblation table.

The third table, the tetrapod, is found in the front central part of the nave [fig. A.69]. It is sometimes called a service table since it is here that several of the sacraments are celebrated: matrimony, baptism, chrismation, as well as other services such as memorial celebrations and thanksgiving services. At the rear in the corners stand two candlesticks with a standing cross in the middle. In front of these are usually found a slightly raised icon box with the icon of the day (feast or saint) and a hand cross of gold or silver placed flat on the tetrapod [figs. A.70, A.71].

When Ukrainians enter a church, they usually go to the tetrapod to venerate the icon and the cross before going to the pews to say their entrance prayers.

Other Important Articles

The epiphation, or shroud (*plashchanytsia*), is a richly decorated

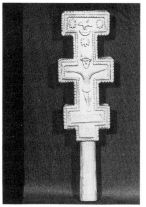

A.69 Tetrapod, Blessed Virgin Mary Church, St. Norbert (L)

A.70 Wooden hand-carved cross found on the tetrapod and used by the priest for blessings, St. Michael Church, Winnipeg (M)

A.71 Hand cross, Holy Ghost Church, Petlura (R)

164

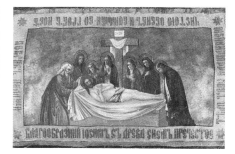

A.72   Epitaphion (or shroud), St. Michael and the Angels Church, Tyndall (L)

A.73   Epitaphion, St. Mary the Protectress Church, Selo Ukraina (R)

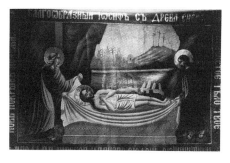

A.74   Epitaphion, St. Michael's Church, Winnipeg (Transcona) (L)

A.75   Epitaphion, St. John the Baptist Church, Caliento (R)

rectangular piece of silk or satin cloth about two feet by four feet [figs. A.72, A.73, A.74, A.75]. On the shroud is an embroidered icon or painted representation of Christ lying in the tomb, and the words of the Hymn of Good Friday are also painted on or embroidered along the four sides.

The epitaphion symbolizes the winding cloth used to wrap Christ's body before He was placed in the tomb. It is brought out on Good Friday and placed on a specially created elevation on the site of the tetrapod. On Holy Saturday it is carried into the sanctuary and placed on the altar. Both celebrations involve processions with the shroud. The Hymn of the Celebration states: "The noble Joseph (of Arimathea), having taken down Thy most holy body from the tree, wrapped it in linen and laid it in a new tomb."

165

Processional banners [figs. A.76, A.77, A.78] are a constant feature of all Ukrainian churches. The banners are usually made of silk or satin, with icons appliquéd to both sides of the banner. Some of the banners are adorned with Ukrainian cross-stitch designs that show the fine needlecraft skills of the women of the parish. Also on occasion the icons are embroidered onto the banners.

In the Ukrainian Church, processions often occur on important feast days. Persons carrying banners precede the priest and the congregation in procession three times around the church. Sometimes the processions are held indoors around the altar.

A large processional cross [figs. A.79, A.80], usually made out of silver or gold, is found in all Ukrainian churches.

The processional cross is carried at the head of all processions.

A censer (*kadylo*) is a special vessel made of bronze or silver; it is suspended on four chains and utilized for burning incense [figs. A.81, A.82, A.83].

A.76   Processional banner (1970s), St. Michael's Church, Gardenton (far L)

A.77   Processional banner (1920s and 1930s), St. Michael's Church, Gardenton (L)

A.78   Processional banners (note the embroidered designs around the icons), Sts. Volodymyr and Olha Church, Gilbert Plains: (a) with icon of Christ; (b) with icon of the Mother of God. (R) (far R)

The censer is symbolic of the gifts offered by the three wise men to the Christ Child: gold, frankincense and myrrh.

A SPECIAL NOTE: THE SHAPE OF THE CROSS

Ukrainians use two forms of crosses in their churches [figs. A.84, A.85, A.86]. The Ukrainian Orthodox use the three-bar cross almost exclusively, while Ukrainian Catholics use the one-bar cross.

The three-bar cross has a special meaning for Ukrainians. The top bar is usually short and has the cyrillic letters "**ІНЦІ**" written on it. The middle bar is the longest and is positioned approximately one-third of the way down the vertical bar. The bottom bar is usually two-thirds of the way down the vertical bar. At one time the bottom bar was parallel to the other two bars. However, over several centuries, this third bar became skewed so that the left side (when one is looking at the cross) is elevated upward and the right side points downward.

The cross is symbolic of the crucifixion of Christ and His suffering and death on it for the sins of the world. Among Ukrainians the cross is also known as a life-giving symbol for, as a result of the

A.79 Processional three-bar cross, St. George's Church, Dauphin (far L)

A.80 Processional one-bar cross, St. Michael's Church, Gardenton (L)

A.81 Censer, St. Michael and the Angels Church, Tyndall (R)

A.82 Censer, St. Mary the Protectress Church, Selo Ukraina (far R)

 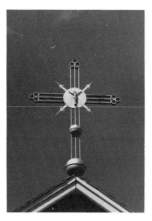 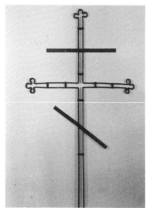 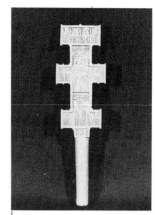

crucifixion, Christ rose on the third day. Thus, often, especially on liturgical days dedicated to it, the cross is decorated with flowers and herbs. It then becomes a symbol of victory over death. Generally, the depiction of Christ on the cross is avoided.

The top bar represents the sign that was nailed above Christ at His crucifixion, bearing the inscription: "Jesus Nazarene, King of the Jews." ("**ІНЦІ**" is the cyrillic transliteration of the Latin inscription "INRI".) [Mark 15:26; Matthew 27:37; Luke 23:38; John 19:19]. The middle bar is the bar on which Christ's hands were nailed.

The bottom bar, the inclined bar, has three symbolic meanings associated with it. First, it is the bar to which Christ's feet were nailed. It is believed that this piece of wood held the weight of the crucified person. The crucifix of Christ usually shows that each foot was nailed to the bar, one on each side of the vertical bar. The inclined position of the bar is a rebuke to those who believe that Christ did not suffer on the cross. His agony was so intense that He wrenched the bar loose when one foot was thrust down and the other was drawn up.

A.83 Censer, Holy Trinity Church, Vita (L)

A.84 Single-bar cross, Blessed Virgin Mary Church, St. Norbert (L)

A.85 Hand-made three-bar cross (1897), Assumption of the Blessed Virgin Mary Church, Ashville (R)

A.86 Carved wooden three-bar cross, St. Michael's Church, Gardenton (R)

Second, the skewed position of the third bar symbolizes the theological destination of the two thieves crucified with Christ. The one on the right asked for forgiveness and repented, while the one on the left blasphemed Christ and was condemned. Thus the one side points upward, in the direction of salvation, while the other points downward, to damnation. Christ's face is turned to the left, parallel to the elevated end of the bar.

Third, the inclined bottom bar makes the cross into a stylized X, or a symbol of the Cross of St. Andrew, the patron saint/apostle of the Ukrainian Church. St. Andrew, according to tradition, visited Kiev, the future site of the capital of Ukraine. Andrew was condemned to death because of his faith in Christ, and asked to be crucified upside down on an X-cross. According to tradition, his wish was granted.

APPENDIX 2:
CONCEPTUAL SCHEME OF THE EVOLUTION OF ARCHITECTURAL STYLES OF UKRAINIAN CHURCHES

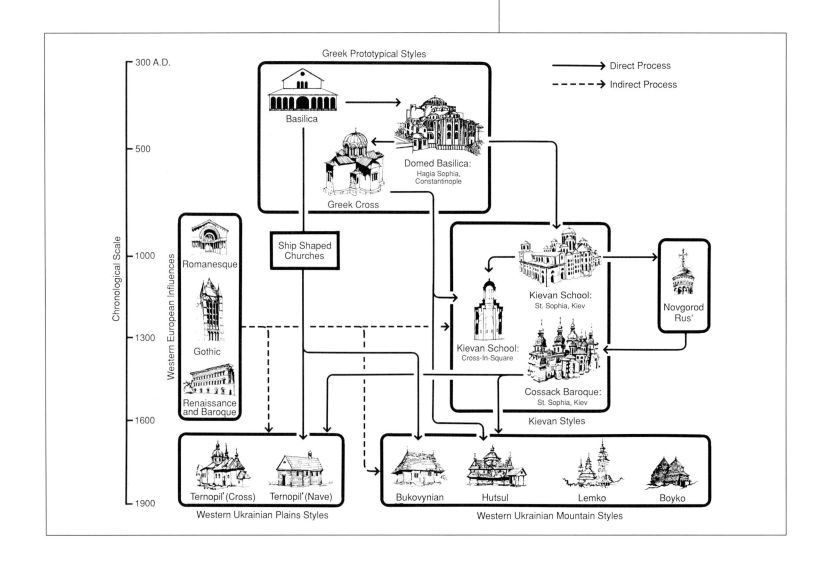

Greek Prototypical Styles

Basilica

Domed Basilica:
Hagia Sophia, Constantinople

Greek Cross

Direct Process
Indirect Process

300 A.D.

500

1000

1300

1600

1900

Chronological Scale

Western European Influences

Romanesque

Gothic

Renaissance and Baroque

Ship Shaped Churches

Kievan School:
St. Sophia, Kiev

Kievan School:
Cross-In-Square

Cossack Baroque:
St. Sophia, Kiev

Kievan Styles

Novgorod Rus'

Ternopil' (Cross)   Ternopil' (Nave)

Western Ukrainian Plains Styles

Bukovynian   Hutsul   Lemko   Boyko

Western Ukrainian Mountain Styles

APPENDIX 3:
WORKS OF THE ARCHITECTS, BUILDERS AND ARTISTS

THE MATERIAL in this appendix is presented for the reader's interest. It lists the works of the artists, architects and builders discussed in chapter 7; it includes as well many additional examples of their work encountered during the research but not treated in this book. It is not, however, a comprehensive list of the creative output of the artists.

Baran, Theodore Artist

Cooks Creek: Immaculate Conception Ukrainian Catholic Church
    (gold-leaf ornamentation)
Mink Creek: Holy Trinity Ukrainian Catholic Church
Neepawa: St. John the Baptist Ukrainian Orthodox Church
Rossburn: Sacred Heart of Jesus Ukrainian Catholic Church
Winnipeg: Our Lady of Perpetual Help Ukrainian Catholic Church

Bartoshuk, Dmytro Artist

Dauphin: St. George's Ukrainian Orthodox Church (sides of
    iconostasis)
Sandy Lake: St. Michael's Ukrainian Orthodox Church
Swan River: Ukrainian Orthodox Church of the Ascension
Winnipeg: Holy Trinity Russian Orthodox Cathedral

Deneka, Victor   Architect

Beausejour: Holy Ghost Ukrainian Catholic Church
East St. Paul: St. Joachim's Ukrainian Catholic Church
Gonor: Holy Trinity Ukrainian Catholic Church (completed Fr. Philip
   Ruh's design)
Portage la Prairie: Ukrainian Catholic Church of the Assumption of the
   Blessed Virgin Mary (third church)
Winnipeg: St. Anne's Ukrainian Catholic Church
Winnipeg: St. Basil's Ukrainian Catholic Church
Winnipeg: Ukrainian Catholic Archdiocese offices
Winnipeg: Ukrainian Catholic Church of the Blessed Virgin Mary

Hordynski, Sviatoslav   Artist

Winnipeg: Holy Eucharist Ukrainian Catholic Church
Winnipeg: St. Mary the Protectress Ukrainian Orthodox Cathedral
   (murals and iconostasis)
Winnipeg: Sts. Vladimir and Olga Ukrainian Catholic Cathedral
   (murals and iconostasis)

Kowal, Roman   Artist

Winnipeg: bas relief of Shevchenko monument
Winnipeg: bas relief sculptures of Ukrainian Catholic Bishops Budka
   and Ladyka
Winnipeg: bas relief, Winnipeg Transit Commission
Winnipeg: Holy Ghost Ukrainian Catholic Church
Winnipeg: St. Michael's Ukrainian Catholic Church
Winnipeg: Sts. Vladimir and Olga Ukrainian Catholic Cathedral
   (stained-glass windows)

Stained glass windows in various churches in Manitoba; paintings and murals in
   Ukrainian churches in Beausejour, Mountain Road, Russell, Winnipeg.

Maydanyk, Jacob   Artist

Dolyny: St. John the Baptist Ukrainian Catholic Church
Fisher Branch: St. Nicholas Ukrainian Catholic Church
Olha: St. Michael's Ukrainian Catholic Church
Winnipeg: Holy Ghost Ukrainian Catholic Church

Paintings and murals in Ukrainian Catholic churches in Meleb, Mountain Road (first
   church), Poplarfield, West Selkirk, Shoal Lake, Rosedale; painting of Bishop Budka
   (held at the Ukrainian Cultural and Educational Centre, Winnipeg).

Mol, Leo   Artist

Brandon: Ukrainian Catholic Church of the Nativity of the Blessed
   Virgin Mary (for Maydanyk)
Winnipeg: Holy Eucharist Ukrainian Catholic Church
Winnipeg: Holy Trinity Ukrainian Orthodox Cathedral (mosaic)
Winnipeg: St. Joseph's Home for the Aged Chapel (stained-glass
   windows)
Winnipeg: St. Jude's Anglican Church (stained-glass windows)
Winnipeg: St. Mary the Protectress Ukrainian Orthodox Cathedral
Winnipeg: Sts. Peter and Paul Ukrainian Catholic Church
Winnipeg: Sts. Vladimir and Olga Ukrainain Catholic Cathedral
   (stained-glass windows)
Winnipeg: Shaarey Zedek Synagogue (stained-glass windows)
Winnipeg: Wentworth United Church (stained-glass windows)

Moroz, Olga (nee Evanchyn) Artist

Seech: Sts. Peter and Paul Ukrainian Orthodox Church (iconostasis)

Paintings in Venlaw and Sandy Lake churches.

Ruh, Fr. Philip Architect and Builder

Clover Leaf: Sts. Peter and Paul Ukrainian Catholic Church
Cooks Creek: grotto of Our Lady of Lourdes
Cooks Creek: Immaculate Conception Ukrainian Catholic Church of
    the Blessed Virgin Mary (formerly St. John the Baptist Church)
Dauphin: Ukrainian Catholic Church of the Resurrection
East Selkirk: Our Lady the Protectress Ukrainian Catholic Church
Gonor: Holy Trinity Ukrainian Catholic Church
Ladywood: Sts. Peter and Paul Ukrainian Catholic Church
Mountain Road: St. Mary's Ukrainian Catholic Church (first church;
    destroyed by fire in 1966)
Portage la Prairie: Ukrainian Catholic Church of the Assumption of the
    Blessed Virgin Mary (second church; demolished in 1983)
Rossdale: Our Lady the Protectress Ukrainian Catholic Church
The Pas: Holy Ghost Ukrainian Catholic Church
West Selkirk: Holy Eucharist Ukrainian Catholic Church
Winnipeg: Holy Eucharist Ukrainian Catholic Church
Winnipegosis: Ukrainian Catholic Church of the Ascension

Sawchuk, Michael Builder

Cooks Creek: bell tower, Immaculate Conception Ukrainian Catholic
    Church of the Blessed Virgin Mary
Gilbert Plains: Sacred Heart of Jesus Ukrainian Catholic Church

Mink Creek: Holy Trinity Ukrainian Catholic Church
Mountain Road: St. Mary's Ukrainian Catholic Church (destroyed by
    fire in 1966)
Ozerna: St. Nicholas Ukrainian Catholic Church
Portage la Prairie: Ukrainian Catholic Church of the Assumption of the
    Blessed Virgin Mary (second church; demolished in 1983)
Sandy Lake: Holy Ghost Ukrainian Catholic Church
Toutes Aides: St. Mary's Ukrainian Catholic Church
Winnipeg: St. Joseph's Ukrainian Catholic Church, residence for
    priests
Winnipegosis: Ukrainian Catholic Church of the Ascension
Zelena: St. Michael's Ukrainian Catholic Church

Numerous halls, houses, tabernacles.

Senchuk, Vera (nee Lazarovich)   Artist

Lennard: Holy Trinity Ukrainian Orthodox Church (iconostasis)

Swystun, Michael   Builder

Rossburn: Sts. Peter and Paul Ukrainian Catholic Church
Seech: St. Mary Ukrainian Catholic Church
Seech: Sts. Peter and Paul Ukrainian Orthodox Church
Solsgirth: Holy Ghost Ukrainian Catholic Church
Vista: Holy Trinity Ukrainian Orthodox Church

Sych, Hnat   Artist

Beausejour: Holy Ghost Ukrainian Catholic Church (first church)
Kosiw: Sts. Peter and Paul Ukrainian Orthodox Church
Poplarfield: Holy Trinity Ukrainian Orthodox Church
Poplarfield: St. Nicholas Ukrainian Catholic Church

Portage la Prairie: Ukrainian Catholic Church of the Assumption of the
    Blessed Virgin Mary (demolished in 1983)
Rosa: Holy Eucharist Urkainian Catholic Church
Stuartburn: Holy Trinity Ukrainian Catholic Church
Vita: Holy Trinity Ukrainian Orthodox Church
Winnipeg: St. Nicholas Ukrainian Catholic Church (demolished ca.
    1966)

Tychaliz, Michael   Builder

Keld: St. Nicholas Ukrainian Catholic Church
Kosiw: Sts. Peter and Paul Ukrainian Orthodox Church

Yanchynski, Michael   Builder

Cooks Creek: Immaculate Conception Ukrainian Catholic Church of
    the Blessed Virgin Mary
Dauphin: Ukrainian Catholic Church of the Resurrection
East Selkirk: Our Lady the Protectress Ukrainian Catholic Church
Mountain Road: St. Mary's Ukrainian Catholic Church (first church;
    destroyed by fire in 1966)
Oakburn: Holy Eucharist Ukrainian Catholic Church
Portage la Prairie: Ukrainian Catholic Church of the Assumption of the
    Blessed Virgin Mary (demolished in 1983)
West Selkirk: Holy Eucharist Ukrainian Catholic Church

The copper domes on Ukrainian Catholic churches in Cooks Creek, Dauphin, Winnipeg.

Zuk, Radoslav   Architect

Tyndall: St. Michael and the Angels Ukrainian Catholic Church
Winnipeg: Holy Family Ukrainian Catholic Church
Winnipeg: St. Joseph's Ukrainian Catholic Church
Winnipeg: St. Michael Ukrainian Catholic Church

APPENDIX 4:
OTHER ARCHITECTS, BUILDERS AND ARTISTS

THE BIOGRAPHIES of some of the architects, builders and artists who made a sizeable artistic and cultural contribution in Manitoba are presented in chapter 7. However, they were not the only ones who did, nor was the contribution of other skilled workers of lesser significance. While doing the research for this book, the authors have come across the names of many others whose skills and talents live on in the Ukrainian churches of Manitoba.

The list of architects and builders who had professional designation prior to 1940 is very short. Those who laboured in the churches before 1940 are listed here in the category that seems to suit their contribution best; if they designed churches, they are considered architects; if they were contractors, supervisors or head carpenters, they are included in the category of builders; if they were involved in the decoration of church interiors either as iconographers or painters, they appear in the category of artists. The list also includes the locations of the churches.

Even though only a preliminary identification has been made at this stage of research, it was deemed appropriate to compile this very tentative list. The authors apologize for any possible gaps. Readers are invited to submit to the authors any revisions or additions that can be documented.

Architects

BROWN, B. St. Nicholas Ukrainian Catholic Church, Winnipeg

DOBUSH, P. St. Andrew's Ukrainian Catholic Church, Winnipeg

G.B.R. ASSOCIATES St. Nicholas Ukrainian Catholic Church, Winnipeg

HEWKI, REV. St. Anthony Petchersky Ukrainian Catholic Church, Lac du Bonnet

NITCHUK, A. St. Nicholas Ukrainian Catholic Church, Winnipeg, Holy Trinity Ukrainian Orthodox Cathedral, Winnipeg

ROBORECKI, REV. Sacred Heart of Jesus Ukrainian Catholic Church, Gilbert Plains

SCHAFER, B. St. Mary's Ukrainian Catholic Church, Mountain Road

Builders

BABITSKYI, Y. Sts. Peter and Paul Ukrainian Catholic Church, Fraserwood

BENDZELIAK, K. Holy Ghost Ukrainian Catholic Church, Winnipeg

BORODY, S. St. Josaphat Ukrainian Catholic Church, Shoal Lake

BURDENIUK, I. and M. St. Michael's Ukrainian Catholic Church, Mink Creek

BURDIE, S. Holy Ghost Ukrainian Catholic Church, Winnipeg

CHALATURNYK, M. St. Michael's Ukrainian Orthodox Church, Gardenton

DAMASKY, Holy Trinity Ukrainian Catholic Church, Stuartburn

DEMKIV, K. St. John the Baptist Ukrainian Catholic Church, Garland

DICKSON, B. Holy Ghost Ukrainian Catholic Church, Solsgirth

DROHOMERESKI, M. and H. St. Stephen the Martyr Ukrainian Orthodox Church, Pleasant Home

FARYMA, S. Assumption Ukrainian Catholic Church, Zhoda

GARCHYNSKYI, J. Ascension of our Lord Jesus Christ Ukrainian Catholic Church, Pulp River

GULEVYCH, V. St. Andrew's Ukrainian Catholic Church, Winnipeg

178

HARASYMCHUK, I. Holy Cross Ukrainian Catholic Church, Inwood
HAWRYSH, M. Holy Eucharist Ukrainian Catholic Church, Horod
HRABCHAK, V. Holy Trinity Ukrainian Catholic Church, Stuartburn
HULOBOCK, A. Ukrainian Catholic Church of the Nativity of the
    Blessed Virgin Mary , Rembrandt
HUMEN, W. The Assumption of our Lord Ukrainian Catholic Church,
    Hadashville
HYKAVY, H. St. John the Baptist Ukrainian Catholic Church, Garland
HYRA, WM. St. Mary's Ukrainian Catholic Church, Russell
ILNYTSKYI, V. Ascension Ukrainian Catholic Church, Sundown
KARPIAH, Holy Trinity Ukrainian Orthodox Church, Vista
KATSAPER, St. Michael's Ukrainian Catholic Church, Venlaw
KHMYLOVSKYI, I. Holy Cross Ukrainian Catholic Church, Pine River
KINIAK, V. Sts. Peter and Paul Ukrainian Catholic Church, Rorketon
KOHUT, I. Sacred Heart Ukrainian Catholic Church, Tolstoi
KOHUT, N. Holy Trinity Ukrainian Catholic Church, Stuartburn
KOLBA, N. The Assumption of our Lord Ukrainian Catholic Church,
    Hadashville; Holy Cross Ukrainian Catholic Church, Elma
KOTOWICH, FR. M. St. Michael and the Angels Ukrainian Catholic
    Church, Tyndall
KLYM, M. and O. Sts. Peter and Paul Ukrainian Catholic Church,
    Thalberg
KOLTUTSKYI, J. and P. St. Michael's Ukrainian Catholic Church, Olha;
    St. John the Baptist Ukrainian Catholic Church, Dolyny; Holy Ghost
    Ukrainian Catholic Church, Angusville
KOVTUN, R. Holy Trinity Ukrainian Catholic Church, Brokenhead
KRUKER, St. John the Baptist Ukrainian Catholic Church, Caliento
KUCH, V. Assumption Ukrainian Catholic Church, Seech
KULAK, S. St. Joachim Ukrainian Catholic Church, East St. Paul
KYKOT, W. St. Michael's Ukrainian Orthodox Church, Gardenton
KYRULUK, P. Holy Eucharist Ukrainian Catholic Church, Rosa
MAGNOWSKI, N. St. Mary's Ukrainian Catholic Church, Russell

MAKARENKO,   St. Joseph's Ukrainian Catholic Church, Winnipeg

MARYKUS, P. Holy Ghost Ukrainian Catholic Church, Winnipeg

MASTKIV, A. Ascension of Our Lord Ukrainian Catholic Church, Petlura

MASYK, S. Holy Cross Ukrainian Catholic Church, Inwood

MELNYK, N. Holy Ghost Ukrainian Catholic Church, Fishing River

MEUSH, S. Holy Eucharist Ukrainian Catholic Church, Oakburn; St. Mary the Protectress Ukrainian Orthodox Cathedral, Winnipeg: St. Michael's Ukrainian Catholic Church, Winnipeg (Transcona)

MNOHOLYTNY, J., St. Volodymyr Ukrainian Orthodox Church, Oakburn

MRYGLOD, A. Transfiguration Ukrainian Catholic Church, Sylvan

NOVOSAD, T. Assumption Ukrainian Catholic Church, Seech; Ascension of Our Lord Ukrainian Catholic Church, Petlura

NAZAREWICH, J. St. Mary's Ukrainian Orthodox Church, Sapton

ONYSCHUK, P. Annunciation of the Blessed Virgin Mary Ukrainian Catholic Church, Skylake

OZARKO, K.M. St. Nicholas Ukrainian Catholic Church, Fisher Branch

PAKULAK, P. St. Stephen the Martyr Ukrainian Orthodox Church, Pleasant Home

PALAMARCHUK, M. St. Demetrius Ukrainian Catholic Church, Ladywood

PALYI, S. Holy Eucharist Ukrainian Catholic Church, Rosa

PANCHUK, J. Holy Transfiguration Ukrainian Orthodox Church, Menzie

PASKIW, P. St. Mary's Ukrainian Catholic Church, Flin Flon

POPOWYCH, I. St. Michael's Ukrainian Catholic Church, Winnipeg (Transcona)

PRYCHUN, A. St. Michael and the Angels Ukrainian Catholic Church, Tyndall; Sts. Peter and Paul Ukrainian Orthodox Church, Tyndall; Sts. Peter and Paul Ukrainian Catholic Church, Glenella; Blessed Virgin Mary the Protectress Ukrainian Catholic Church, Glenhope; St. Elias Ukrainian Orthodox Church, Sirko

PRYGROTSKY, H. Holy Trinity Ukrainian Catholic Church, Stuartburn

RACHUK, S. St. Michael's Ukrainian Catholic Church, Winnipeg (Transcona)

RHYHOR, P. St. Stephen the Martyr Ukrainian Orthodox Church, Pleasant Home

ROMANCHUK, O. Holy Family Ukrainian Catholic Church, Winnipeg

RURAK, O. St. Demetrius Ukrainian Catholic Church, Drifting River

SAMEC, J. The Assumption of Our Lord Ukrainian Catholic Church, Hadashville

SAWATSKY CONSTRUCTION LTD. St. Mary's Ukrainian Catholic Church, Mountain Road

SEMKO, P. Holy Eucharist Ukrainian Catholic Church, Selkirk

SENKO, S. Blessed Virgin Mary the Protectress Ukrainian Catholic Church, Rosedale

SHMOROVSKYI, T. Protection of the Blessed Virgin Mary Ukrainian Catholic Church, Malonton

SIDORYK, M.J. St. Mary's Ukrainian Catholic Church, Russell

SKRYNSKYI, P. Holy Eucharist Ukrainian Catholic Church, Rosa

SKRYPKA, J. Blessed Virgin Mary the Protectress Ukrainian Catholic Church, East Selkirk

URBANOVYCH, P. St. Stephen the Martyr Ukrainian Orthodox Church, Pleasant Home

YAVORSKYI, A. Sts. Peter and Paul Ukrainian Catholic Church, Valley River; Assumption of the Blessed Virgin Mary Ukrainian Catholic Church, Kulish; St. John the Baptist Ukrainian Catholic Church, Fork River

ZABOLOTSKYI, H. Assumption of the Blessed Virgin Mary Ukrainian Catholic Church, Meleb

In addition, the following builders have been identified, but the names and locations of their work are uncertain: Penchak, L., Prokopovych, I., Stecura, I., Tanasichuk, J.

Artists

KOSTUR, B. St. Michael's Ukrainian Catholic Church, Winnipeg
   (Transcona)
PATCHOWSKY, R. Sts. Vladimir and Olga Ukrainian Catholic
   Cathedral, Winnipeg
SUHACEV, I. Holy Ghost Ukrainian Catholic Church, Beausejour;
   Transfiguration Ukrainian Catholic Church, Roblin; St. Joseph's
   Ukrainian Catholic Church, Winnipeg
WOLANIUK, J. Sts. Vladimir and Olga Ukrainian Catholic Cathedral,
   Winnipeg

APPENDIX 5:
LOCATIONS OF CHURCHES

Eastern and southeastern regions

Holy Eucharist Ukrainian Catholic Church, Rosa, 70 km. south of Winnipeg on PTH 59

Holy Ghost Ukrainian Catholic Church, Beausejour, 48 km. northeast of Winnipeg on PTH 44

Holy Trinity Ukrainian Catholic Church, Stuartburn, 85 km. south of Winnipeg, off PTH 59 east on PR 201

Holy Trinity Ukrainian Catholic Church, Gonor, 20 km. north of Winnipeg, on PR 204 (Henderson Highway)

Immaculate Conception Ukrainian Catholic Church, Cooks Creek, 8 km. east of Birds Hill Provincial Park, on PR 212

Sacred Heart Ukrainian Catholic Church, Tolstoi, 86 km. south of Winnipeg on PTH 59

St. Anthony Petchersky Ukrainian Catholic Church, Lac du Bonnet, 110 km. northeast of Winnipeg, on PTH 11

St. Elias Ukrainian Orthodox Church, Sirko, 25 km. south of PTH 12, on PR 402, 1 1/2 km. north of the United States border

St. Michael and the Angels Ukrainian Catholic Church, Tyndall, 35 km. northeast of Winnipeg on PTH 44

St. Michael's Ukrainian Orthodox Church, Gardenton, 95 km. southeast of Winnipeg, off PTH 59

Sts. Peter and Paul Ukrainian Catholic Church, Clover Leaf, 3 km. east of PTH 12, on Hazelridge Road (east of Birds Hill Provincial Park)

Interlake region

Holy Trinity Ukrainian Orthodox Church, Poplarfield, 116 km. north of Winnipeg, on PTH 17

St. Demetrius Ukrainian Orthodox Church, Camp Veselka, 7 km. north of Gimli, east off PTH 8 or 9

St. Nicholas Ukrainian Catholic Church, Poplarfield, 116 km. north of Winnipeg, on PTH 17

St. Volodymyr Ukrainian Catholic Chapel, Ukrainian Park at Camp Morton, 11 km. north of Gimli, east off PTH 8 or 9

Ukrainian Catholic Church of the Nativity of the Blessed Virgin Mary, Rembrandt, 93 km. north of Winnipeg on PTH 7

Riding Mountain National Park region

Ascension of Our Lord Ukrainian Catholic Church, Petlura, 15 km. south of PTH 5, just north of Riding Mountain National Park

Ascension of Our Lord Ukrainian Catholic Church, Ukraina, 50 km. north of Dauphin, off PTH 10

Assumption of the Blessed Virgin Mary Ukrainian Catholic Church, Ashville, 3 km. east of PTH 10, in the Ashville area, about 15 km. west of Dauphin

Holy Ghost Ukrainian Orthodox Church, Petlura, 11 km. south of PTH 5, north of Riding Mountain National Park

Holy Resurrection Orthodox Church, Sifton, 30 km. north of Dauphin on PR 362

Holy Trinity Ukrainian Orthodox Church, Valley River, 12 km. northwest of Dauphin on PR 362

St. Elie Romanian/Ukrainian Orthodox Church, Lennard, west of Riding Mountain National Park, south of Roblin, 8 km. east of PTH 83

St. George's Ukrainian Orthodox Church, 804 Main Street South, Dauphin

St. John the Baptist Ukrainian Catholic Church, Dolyny, 10 km. north of Menzie, off PTH 45

St. Josaphat Ukrainian Catholic Church, Shoal Lake, 60 km. west of Minnedosa on PTH 16 (the Yellowhead)

St. Michael's Ukrainian Catholic Church, Mink Creek, 60 km. northwest of Dauphin, 10 km. west of PTH 10

St. Michael's Ukrainian Catholic Church, Olha, 10 km. north of Oakburn, off PR 566

St. Michael's Ukrainian Orthodox Church, Sandy Lake, 255 km northwest of Winnipeg on PTH 16 (the Yellowhead), just south of Riding Mountain National Park

St. Volodymyr Ukrainian Orthodox Church, Oakburn, 14 km. north of Shoal Lake, off PTH 16 (the Yellowhead)

Sts. Peter and Paul Ukrainian Catholic Church, Glenella, 11 km. north of Glenella and 1 km. east (Glenella is 40 km. north of PTH 16 [the Yellowhead], past the town of Gladstone)

Sts. Peter and Paul Ukrainian Orthodox Church, Seech, 30 km. north of PTH 16, on PR 470

Transfiguration Ukrainian Orthodox Church, Pine River, 80 km. north of Dauphin on PTH 10

Ukrainian Catholic Church of the Ascension, Winnipegosis, 50 km. north of Dauphin on PTH 20

Ukrainian Catholic Church of the Holy Ghost, Merridale, 22 km. north of Roblin, off PR 483

Ukrainian Catholic Church of the Resurrection, 17 Eleventh Avenue S.W., Dauphin

Ukrainian Orthodox Church of the Ascension, Angusville, 19 km. west of Russell, off PTH 45

Ukrainian Orthodox Church of the Transfiguration, Menzie, 12 km. north of PTH 16 (the Yellowhead), south of Riding Mountain National Park

Winnipeg

All Saints Ukrainian Orthodox Church, 1500 Day Street

Holy Family Ukrainian Catholic Church, 1001 Grant Avenue

Holy Ghost Ukrainian Catholic Church, 1954 Logan Avenue

Holy Transfiguration Independent Greek Church, 193 McGregor Street

Holy Trinity Ukrainian Orthodox Cathedral, 1175 Main Street

St. Joseph's Ukrainian Catholic Church, 250 Jefferson Avenue

St. Mary the Protectress Ukrainian Orthodox Cathedral, 820 Burrows Avenue

St. Michael Ukrainian Orthodox Church, 110 Disraeli

St. Nicholas Ukrainian Catholic Church, 737 Bannerman Avenue

Sts. Vladimir and Olga Cathedral Ukrainian Catholic Cathedral, 115 McGregor Street

Ukrainian Greek Orthodox Cathedral of St. John Suchavsky, 931 Main Street

NOTES

Preface

1. The Manitoba East European Heritage Society is a community group
   founded in 1983 by three university professors who were concerned with
   the preservation, documentation and fostering of the knowledge about the
   cultural heritage of Manitobans of Ukrainian and eastern European descent.

Chapter 1

1. This as well is a reflection of the fact that many of the early Manitoba
   Ukrainian settlers originated from today's Ternopil' region.

Chapter 2

1. D. Talbot Rice, *Byzantine Art* (Harmondsworth: Penguin Books, 1962), p. 84.
2. In all likelihood the taller drum was a local adaptation in response to the
   need for increased window area. Kievan domes were somewhat narrower
   than the Byzantine prototypes, but more light had to be admitted to provide adequate lighting in a more northern latitude.
3. Majolica plates are a form of glazed clay tile, used for the decoration of masonry buildings.
4. *Hetman* is the name given to elected Ukrainian Cossack rulers.
5. George Korbyn, *Ukrainian Style in Church Architecture* (Acadia: Korbyn,
   1983), p. 33.

Chapter 3

1. The churches featured in this chapter do not represent all the architectural
   variations found in Ukraine, nor do they encompass all the regions. They
   have been described selectively to focus on those styles that are more
   commonly found among Ukrainian churches in Manitoba, and that are the
   subject of chapter 4.

2. Timber framing is a method of construction in which the major structural members are set vertically at regular intervals, with lighter materials filling the spaces. Timber laying is a method in which the members are stacked horizontally, as in a log cabin.

Chapter 4

1. St. Mary the Protectress has traditionally been considered the patron of the Cossacks.
2. It is reported that on that day very strong winds were blowing through the spaces between the logs, and the women had to go outside and collect moss to fill the spaces.
3. St. Michael's Ukrainian Orthodox Church in Gardenton was declared a provincial heritage site under the Heritage Resources Act in 1974.
4. St. Elie Romanian/Ukrainian Orthodox Church in Lennard was declared a provincial heritage site under the Heritage Resources Act in 1986.

Chapter 5

1. The Immaculate Conception Ukrainian Catholic Church in Cooks Creek was declared a provincial heritage site under the Heritage Resources Act in 1986.

Chapter 6

1. St. Michael and the Angels Church in Tyndall is to be destroyed in 1990.

Chapter 7

1. See appendix 3 for an alphabetical list of the architects, builders and artists whose biographical sketches are included in this chapter. Along with each name is a list, arranged with the location appearing first, of the churches he or she worked on. The list does not include all the churches associated with each architect, builder or artist, but rather includes all the churches encountered in the research.
2. A book-length biography of Ruh is currently being written by Gloria Romaniuk of Cooks Creek, Manitoba.

3. The church in Portage la Prairie was built between 1926 and 1928; the one in Dauphin [fig. 4.2] between 1936 and 1938; and the one in Cooks Creek [fig. 5.16] between 1930 and 1940.
4. Radoslav Zuk, untitled article, n.d.
5. "Leo Mol Exhibits at the Gallery," Winnipeg Art Gallery news release, September 24, 1974.
6. "Stained Glass in the Cathedral of Sts. Vladimir and Olga in Winnipeg," pamphlet, author and publisher unknown, n.d.
7. Questionnaire completed by Olga Moroz, December 1986.

BIBLIOGRAPHY

Published Sources

Baggley, J. *Doors of Perception.* Crestwood: St. Vladimir's Seminary Press, 1988.

Bazhan, M.P. (ed) *Istoriia Ukrains'koho Mystetstva.* Vol. 6 of 7 vols. Kyïv: Akademiia Nauk Ukrainskoi SSR, 1966 – 1968.

Bouyer, L. *Liturgy and Architecture.* Notre Dame: University of Notre Dame Press, 1967.

Brumfield, W.C. *Gold in Azure: One Thousand Years of Russian Architecture.* Boston: David R. Godine Publ. Inc., 1983.

Buxton, D. *The Wooden Churches of Eastern Europe.* Cambridge: Cambridge University Press, 1981.

Department of Cultural Affairs and Historic Resources. *Early Architecture of Portage la Prairie, Manitoba.* Winnipeg: Province of Manitoba, 1983.

Department of Culture, Heritage and Recreation, Historic Resources Branch. *Ukrainian Churches of Manitoba: A Building Inventory.* Winnipeg: Province of Manitoba, 1987.

Derev'iani Tserkvy v Ukraini [Wooden Churches in Ukraine]. Toronto: "My i svit," Publishers, 1956.

Doroshenko, D. *History of the Ukraine.* Edmonton: The Institute Press, 1939.

Ewanchuk, M. *Spruce, Swamp and Stone: A History of the Pioneer Ukrainian Settlements in the Gimli Area.* Winnipeg: M. Ewanchuk, 1977.

_____. *Pioneer Settlers: Ukrainians in the Dauphin Area 1896 – 1926.* Winnipeg: M. Ewanchuk, 1988.

Frankl, P. *Gothic Architecture.* Harmondsworth: Penguin, 1962.

Froncek, T., ed. *The Horizon Book of the Arts of Russia.* New York: American Heritage Publishing Co., 1970.

Hewryk, T.D. *The Lost Architecture of Kiev.* New York: The Ukrainian Museum, 1982.

_____. *Derev'iani Khramy Ukrainy.* New York: The Ukrainian Museum, 1987.

Himka, J.P. "Priests and Peasants: The Uniate Factor and the Ukrainian National Movement in Austria, 1867 – 1900." *Canadian Slavonic Papers* 21 (March 1979): 1 – 14.

Hoddinott, R.F. *Early Byzantine Churches in Macedonia and Southern Serbia.* London: Macmillan, 1963.

Hohn, H., ed. *Byzantine Churches of Alberta*. Edmonton: The Edmonton Art Gallery, 1976.

Hordynsky, S. *The Ukrainian Icon of the Twelfth to Eighteenth Centuries*. Philadelphia: Providence Association, 1973.

Hoshko, Iu. H., ed. *Boikivshchyna: Istoryko-Etnohrafichne Doslidzhennia*. Kyïv: Naukova dumka, 1983.

Hoshko, Iu.H., et al. *Narodna Arkhitektura Ukrains'kykh Karpat XV– XX st*. Kyïv: Naukova Dumka, 1987.

Hrushevsky, M. *A History of Ukraine*. New Haven: Yale University Press, 1941.

Hryniuk, S. "A Peasant Society in Transition: Ukrainian Peasants in Five East Galician Counties, 1880 – 1900." Ph.D. dissertation, University of Manitoba, 1985.

Hryniuk, S., and Yereniuk, R. "Building the New Jerusalem on the Prairies: The Ukrainian Experience." In Smillie, B., ed. *Visions of The New Jerusalem: Religious Settlement on the Prairies*. Edmonton: NeWest Press, 1983.

Humeniuk, P. *Hardships and Progress of Ukrainian Pioneers*. Steinbach: Derksen Printers, 1976.

Ilarion (Ohienko), Metropolitan. *Ikonoborstvo [Iconoclasm]*. Winnipeg: Ukrainian Orthodox Church of Canada, 1954.

Iurchenko, P.H. *Dereviana Arkhitektura Ukrainy [The Wooden Architecture of Ukraine]*. Kyïv: "Budivel'nyk," 1970.

Jones, L.E. *The Observer's Handbook of Old English Churches*. London: Frederick Warne and Co. Ltd., 1984.

Karger, M.K. *Arkheologicheskiie Issledovaniia Drevnego Kieva*. Kyïv: Academiia Nauk Ukrainskoi SSR, 1951.

Karmazyn-Kakovs'ky, V. *Mystetstvo Lemkivs'koi Tserkvy (De Arte Sacra Ecclesiarum Lemcoviensium)*. Rome: Ukrainian Catholic University of St. Clement, 1975.

_____. *Arkhitektura Boikivs'koi Tserkvy*. New York: Boikivshchyna Society, 1987.

Kaye, V.J. *Early Ukrainian Settlements in Canada, 1895 – 1900*. Toronto: University of Toronto Press, 1964.

Kolokyris, C.D. *The Essence of Orthodox Iconography*. Brookline: Holy Cross School of Theology, 1971.

Korbyn, George. *Ukrainian Style in Church Architecture*. Arcadia: Korbyn, 1983.

Krautheimer, R. *Early Christian and Byzantine Architecture*. New York: Penguin, 1986.

Kresal'nyi, N.I. *Sofiysky Monument-Museum of Kiev*. Kiev: State Publishing House of Building and Architecture Literature of the Ukrainian SSR, 1962.

Kronquist, E.F. *Metalwork for Craftsmen.* New York: Dover Publications, 1972.

Kubijovic, V., ed. *Encyclopedia of Ukraine.* Toronto: University of Toronto Press, Toronto, 1984.

_____. *Ukraine: A Concise Encyclopedia.* Toronto: University of Toronto Press, 1963.

Ledohowski, E.M., and Butterfield, D.K. *Architectural Heritage: The Eastern Interlake Planning District.* Winnipeg: Department of Cultural Affairs and Historic Resources, Province of Manitoba, 1983.

Lehr, J.C. "The Process and Pattern of Ukrainian Settlement in Western Canada." Ph.D. dissertation, University of Manitoba, 1978.

Lew, W. et al., eds. *The Tchortkiv District: A Collection of Memoirs and Historic Data.* Toronto: Executive Committee of the Tchortkiv District Countrymen, 1974.

Lohvyn, H.N. *Po Ukraini; Starodavni Mystets'ki Pam'iatky.* Kyїv: "Mystetstvo," 1968.

_____. *Kiev's St. Sophia Architectural-Historical Monument.* Kiev: "Mystetstvo," 1971.

Lupul, M., ed. *A Heritage in Transition: Essays in the History of Ukrainians in Canada.* Toronto: McClelland and Stewart, 1982.

MacDonald, W. *Early Christian and Byzantine Architecture.* New York: Braziller, 1982.

Magocsi, P.R. *Ukraine: A Historical Atlas.* Toronto: Universtity of Toronto Press, 1985.

Makushenko, P.I., and Petrova, Z.A. *Narodnaia Arkhitektura Zakarpat'ia.* Kiev: Gosstroiizdat UkSSR, 1956.

Margo, C. *Byzantine Architecture.* New York: Harry N. Abrams, Inc., 1976.

Marunchak, M.H. *Studies in the History of Ukrainians in Canada.* Vol 2. Winnipeg: Ukrainian Free Academy of Sciences, 1967.

_____. *The Ukrainian Canadians: A History.* Winnipeg: Ukrainian Academy of Arts and Sciences, 1982.

Ouspensky, L. *Theology of the Icon.* Crestwood: St. Vladimir's Seminary Press, 1978.

Ouspensky, L., and Lossky, V. *The Meaning of Icons.* Crestwood: St. Vladimir's Seminary Press, 1982.

Papioannou, K. *Byzantine and Russian Painting.* New York: Funk and Wagnall, 1965.

Petrenko, M.Z., ed. *Kievo-Pechers'kyi Derzhavnyi Istoryko-Kul'turnyi Zapovidnyk [A Short Guide, Ministry of Culture, Ukrainian SSR]*. Kyïv: "Mystetstvo," 1981.

Petryshyn, R., ed. *Changing Realities: Social Trends Among Ukrainian Canadians*. Edmonton: Canadian Institute of Ukrainian Studies, 1980.

Powstenko, O. *The Cathedral of Saint Sophia*. New York: Ukrainian Academy of Arts and Science, 1954.

Propamiatna Knyha z Nahody Zolotoho Iuvileiu Poselennia Ukrainskoho Narodu v Kanadi. Yorkton, Sask: Holos Spasytelia, 1941.

Romaniuk, G., ed. *Reverend Philip Ruh, O.M.I.: Missionary and Architect*. Cooks Creek: Parish of the Church of the Immaculate Conception, 1984.

Runciman, S. *Byzantine Style and Civilization*. New York: Meridian Books, 1956.

St. Theodore the Studite. *On Holy Icons*. Translated by C.P. Roth. Crestwood: St. Vladimir's Seminary Press, 1981.

Sichyns'ki, V. *Pamiatky Ukrainskoi Arkhitektury [Monuments of Ukrainian Architecture]*. Philadelphia: "America," 1952.

Talbot Rice, D. *Byzantine Art*. Rev. ed. Harmondsworth: Penguin Books, 1962.

Talbot Rice, T. *A Concise History of Russian Art*. New York: Praeger, 1967.

_____. *Russian Art*. West Drayton, Middlesex: Penguin Books, 1949.

Trubetskoi, E.N. *Icons: Theology in Color*. Crestwood: St. Vladimir's Seminary Press, 1973.

Tsyakalovs'kyi, O. *Starovynni pam'iatky Volyni*. Toronto: Volyn', 1975.

Untracht, O. *Metal Techniques for Craftsmen*. New York: Doubleday, 1968.

Van Milligen, A. *Byzantine Churches in Constantinople*. London: Macmillan, 1912.

Volbach, W.F., and Lafontaine-Dosogne, J., eds. *Byzanz und der Christliche Osten*. Propyläen Kunstgeschichte, Band 3. Berlin: Propyläen Verlag, 1968.

Yuzyk, P. *Ukrainians in Manitoba*. Toronto: University of Toronto Press, 1953.

Zapletal, F. *Wooden Churches in the Carpathians*. Wien: W. Braumüller, 1982.

Other Sources

Interviews and correspondence with: T. Baran, D. Bartoshuk, T. Koshowski, K. Kuzyk, Emil Michaels, W. Michalchyshyn, L. Mol, O. Moroz, G. Romaniuk, J. Slogan, M. Yanchynsky, R. Zuk.

Films, National Film Board: "The Strongest Man on Earth," and "Laughter in my Soul," produced by Halya Kuchmij.

Numerous local and parish histories.

INDEX

Mountain Road 114; St. Mary's Church 107
Muscovy 3, 30

Nativity *See* Church of the Nativity, Palestine; Ukrainian Catholic Church of the Nativity of the Blessed Virgin Mary, Rembrandt; Church of the Nativity of the Virgin Mary, Zubov
Nicholas *See* St. Nicholas Ukrainian Catholic Church, Poplarfield; St. Nicholas Church, Terebovlia; St. Nicholas Ukrainian Catholic Church, Winnipeg
Nitchuk, Alex 98, 100, 178
Novgorod 26
Novosad, Theodore 77

Oakburn 8, 11, 112, 114; Holy Eucharist Church 141, 145, 150, 159, 163; St. Volodymyr Ukrainian Orthodox Church 85
Olha, St. Michael's Ukrainian Catholic Church 86
opasannia 37, 39, 40, 41, 55, 60, 65
Ottoman Empire 3

Pachowsky, R. 103
Palestine, Church of the Holy Sepulchre 18; Church of the Nativity 18
Pankevych, Julian 115
Panteleimon, St. *See* Church of St. Panteleimon, Halych
Pantheon 18
Papadakis, Kostas 85
Paulenko, John 64
Peremyshl' 28

Peter and Paul, Sts. *See* Sts. Peter and Paul Ukrainian Catholic Church, Clover Leaf; Sts. Peter and Paul Ukrainian Catholic Church, Glenella; Sts. Peter and Paul Ukrainian Orthodox Church, Seech
Petlura, Ascension of our Lord Ukrainian Catholic Church 77; Holy Ghost Ukrainian Orthodox Church 87, 164
piddashshia 15, 37, 39, 40, 60
Pidstawka, Mr. 51
Pine River, Transfiguration Ukrainian Orthodox Church 47
Poberezhzhia 28
Poland (Polish) 3, 28, 30, 32, 35, 76; people 36
Poltava 76
Poplarfield, Holy Trinity Ukrainian Orthodox Church 62; St. Nicholas Ukrainian Catholic Church 57
Popoff, Fr. Constantine 56
Portage la Prairie 8, 113; Church of the Assumption of the Blessed Virgin Mary 13, 108, 113, 135, 136
Powstenko, Alexander 100
prairie cathedrals (Fr. Ruh's) 15, 107
Pratt and Ross 100
Protestant 11, 94
Prychun, Anton 72

Rembrandt, Ukrainian Catholic Church of the Nativity of the Blessed Virgin Mary 55
Resurrection *See* Ukrainian Catholic Church of the Resurrection, Dauphin; Holy Resurrection Orthodox Church, Sifton
Riding Mountain National Park 8

Roborets'ky, Fr. Andrew 46
Romanesque 28, 57, 89
Romania (Romanian) 3, 35, 64
Rome (Roman): architecture 21; basilica 17; Empire 18; Pantheon 18
Rosa, Holy Eucharist Ukrainian Catholic Church 83, 158, 161
Roseau River 56
Ruh, Fr. Philip 15, 46, 69, 71, 76, 89, 91, 93, 106–108, 109, 111, 112, 113, 174
Rus': Kievan 1, 17, 21, 28, 30, 33; Novgorod 26; sub-Carpathian 35
Russia (Russian): Church 32; Empire 10, 32; influence 10; Orthodox mission 50, 52, 56, 75, 95
Rymiak, Dmytro 77

Sacred Heart Ukrainian Catholic Church, Tolstoi 62
Safriuk, Mr. and Mrs. 94
St. Andrew's Church, Winnipeg 124
St. Anthony Petchersky Ukrainian Catholic Church, Lac du Bonnet 87
St. Demetrius Ukrainian Orthodox Church, Camp Veselka (formerly in Malonton) 66, 153
St. Elias Ukrainian Orthodox Church, Sirko 65, 159
St. Elie Romanian/Ukrainian Orthodox Church, Lennard 64
St. George's Ukrainian Orthodox Church, Dauphin 83, 143, 167
St. John the Baptist Church, Caliento 140, 141, 153, 154, 163, 165; Dry River 160
St. John the Baptist Ukrainian Catholic Church, Dolyny 72